Welcome to LifeSearch!

If you urgently need to prepare to lead a LifeSearch group, turn the page and read QuickLead®. QuickLead® will give you enough information to get started.

LifeSearch hopes to help you and other persons within a small group explore topics about which you are concerned in your everyday living. We've tried to make LifeSearch

✓ immediately helpful to you;

✓ filled with practical ideas;

✓ Christian-oriented and biblically based;

✓ group building, so you will find companions in your mutual struggles and learning;

✓ easy for anyone to lead.

You have probably chosen to join with others in studying this LifeSearch book because you feel some need. You may feel that need in your life strongly. Our hope for you is that by the time you complete the six chapters in this book with your LifeSearch group, you will have

✓ a better handle on how to meet the need you feel;

✓ some greater insights into yourself;

✓ a deeper understanding of how Christian faith can help you meet that need;

✓ a more profound relationship with God;

✓ new and/or richer relationships with the other persons in your LifeSearch group.

If you discover nothing else as part of this LifeSearch experience, we want you to learn this fact: *that you are not alone as you face life*. Other people have faced and still face the same problems, struggles, demands, and needs that you face. Some have advice to offer. Some have learned things the hard way—things they can now tell you about. Some can help you think through and talk through old concerns and new insights. Some can listen as you share what you've tried and what you want to achieve. Some even need what you can offer.

And you will never be alone because God stands with you.

The secret to LifeSearch is in the workings of your group. No two LifeSearch groups will ever be alike. Your LifeSearch group is made up of unique individuals—including you. All of you have much to offer one another. This LifeSearch book simply provides a framework for you and your group to work together in learning about an area of mutual concern.

IF YOU ARE LEADING A LifeSearch GROUP, please read the articles in the back of this book. These LifeSearch group leadership articles may answer the questions you have about leading your group.

IF YOU ARE PARTICIPATING IN A LifeSearch GROUP, BUT NOT LEADING IT, please read at least the article "If You're Not Leading the Group." In any case, **you will benefit most if you come to your group meeting having read the chapter ahead of time and having attempted any assignments given in the previous chapter's "Before Next Time" sections.**

We want to remain helpful to you throughout your LifeSearch group experience. If you have any questions about using this LifeSearch book, please feel free to call Curric-U-Phone at 1-800-251-8591 and ask for the LifeSearch editor.

QUICKLEAD®

Look here for **QUICK** information about how to **LEAD** a session of LIFE-SEARCH. On LIFESEARCH pages, look for the following:

ICONS
Seven kinds of icons suggest different kinds of activities for your group to do at different points during the session (see page 4 for more information about ICONS).

MAIN TEXT: the "meat" of the session. Hopefully everyone will have read the MAIN TEXT ahead of time; if not, be prepared to offer a brief summary of the MAIN TEXT in your own words.

MARGINAL NOTES give you activity instructions and additional discussion starters.

CHAPTER THREE

RELATIONSHIPS: THE PULL BETWEEN INTIMACY AND ISOLATION

CHECKING IN
What is happening in your life that you want the group to know about?

Tell about an intimate relationship in your life. What makes it so special?

DISCUSSION POINT
How would you define an intimate relationship?

DISCUSSION POINT
How would you define a "differentiated" person?

Examine our tendency to want our mate to think and act "just like me."

How can we take Dowrick's suggestion and approach an intimate relationship in a state of "not knowing"? Why might this enhance the aliveness of a relationship?

DEALING WITH CHANGE

Creating Intimate Relationships

This chapter shifts the focus from relationships within our family of origin to intimate relationships we create in our adult world. As adults, we yearn for meaningful attachments. Intimate relationships can provide us with a feeling of connection, of being fully alive. An intimate relationship provides us with the opportunity to mutually share our hopes and dreams, our fears and pains, our joys and sorrows. While no relationship can meet all our needs, we long for a special partner who affirms us and with whom we can experience the aliveness found in giving and receiving love.

An enduring relationship requires movement from being a fairly immature, undifferentiated person to a more mature person who has a sense of self, accepts responsibility for one's actions, and is able to tolerate the give and take of life with another distinctive human being. Less-healthy relationships struggle against the tendency for one's mate to grow and change; differences in thoughts, interests, and feelings are viewed as a threat. Not comfortable with a more unique or "differentiated" companion, partners employ blame, guilt, and manipulation to maintain a more "fused" relationship.[1]

In contrast, Stephanie Dowrick suggests we enhance the aliveness of our intimate relationship by approaching our mate in a state of "not knowing." "Otherwise you've shut your eyes to that person's constant processes of change."[2] While our past forms a significant part of our identity, our present experiences and feelings plus our future dreams compose significant parts of our constantly changing identity.

Fueled by a fear that being different will weaken the relationship, immature couples become more and more isolated, trapped in roles that no longer fit. The relationship stagnates. If either partner is uncomfortable with this arrangement, the only possibility for growth is viewed as occurring outside the relationship. Alternatively, in a more mature relationship, difference, otherness, unpredictability, and change are accepted as necessary to ensure a level of vitality and enjoyment for the persons as individuals and as a couple.

21

UNDERLINED TEXT identify discussion starters inside the MAIN TEXT.

For more information, read the **LEADERSHIP ARTICLES** in the back of this LIFESEARCH book.

DEALING WITH CHANGE

ICONS

ICONS are picture/symbols that show you at a glance what you should do with different parts of the main text at different times in the LIFESEARCH sessions.

The seven kinds of icons are

WORSHIP—A prayer, hymn, or other act of worship is suggested at this place in the MAIN TEXT.

CHECKING IN—At the beginning of each session, LIFESEARCH group members will be asked to "check in" with one another about what is happening in their lives. Sometimes group members will also be asked to "check in" about how their LIFESEARCH group experience seems to them.

DISCUSSION POINT—Either the MAIN TEXT or a MARGINAL NOTE will suggest discussion starters. You will probably find more DISCUSSION POINTS than you can use in the usual LIFESEARCH session.

GROUP INTERACTION—Either the MAIN TEXT or a MARGINAL NOTE will suggest a group activity that goes beyond a simple discussion within the whole group.

BIBLE STUDY—At least once each session, your LIFESEARCH group will study a Bible passage together. Usually, DISCUSSION POINTS and/or GROUP INTERACTIONS are part of the BIBLE STUDY.

WRITTEN REFLECTION—The MAIN TEXT will contain one or more suggestions for individuals to reflect personally on an issue. Space will be provided within the MAIN TEXT for writing reflections. Sometimes individuals will be invited to share their written reflections if they wish.

BEFORE NEXT TIME—In most sessions, your LIFESEARCH group members will be asked to do something on their own before the next time you meet together.

INTRODUCTION

This volume of LifeSearch will help you explore the nature of change, how it impacts your life, and possible responses to the discontinuities you encounter. That we experience constant change is a given. The question is how we can respond most effectively to the transitions in our life.

The oft-quoted "Serenity Prayer" speaks of the need to "accept the things I cannot change; courage to change the things I can; and wisdom to know the difference."[1] Acceptance of upheavals in our life is necessary, but this study will challenge you to focus on developing the courage to actively respond to the changes you experience.

Some parts of the road of life have breathtakingly beautiful vistas and promise wonderful adventures, while other sections appear icy or full of potholes. To blindly ignore change can result in missing a "curve" sign or "construction ahead" sign. While you do not have total control, you are responsible for how effectively you manage the changes encountered on the road. Do you have a strategy for coping? Whom do you want with you on your journey? Do you experience God by your side?

As a psychologist in private practice, I view myself as a "professional change agent." Each day struggling persons seek counseling as they strive to manage the changes in their life. I am awed by encounters with persons, bent over with pain and suffering, who courageously pick up the pieces of their life and begin new adventures. To walk with them for a while on their journey is a personal and professional privilege. I rejoice when I can share tools and insights that lighten persons' loads, and frequently I am the learner, witnessing gallant efforts and creative solutions.

God's gifts for assisting us to understand change include the insights of the social sciences, such as psychology. This study book draws on these resources with the hope that individuals will use the best knowledge and information available. Christian faith, enriched with our learnings from human experience, can enable persons to transcend the often painful disadvantages of rapid personal and social change and to discover the unexpected, joyful advantages of a new situation or stage in life.

The first chapter of Dealing With Change seeks to broaden our understanding of change. Opportunities and obstacles presented by various discontinuities are examined, and specific qualities that aid in coping with transitions are identified. Inevitable changes in families provide the focus of chapter two. Rather than focusing on families with young children, the second half of the chapter looks at life with adult children. Our need for intimate relationships and the potential for isolation are examined in the third chapter. Chapter four highlights the instability of the world of work and encourages us to increased flexibility and to realistic appraisals of our work situation. Moving also has the potential to be a traumatic experience in persons' lives. Chapter five offers helpful guidelines to deal with feelings of "dislocation." While there are many other challenges meriting discussion, the need to develop care for oneself while coping with a variety of changes seems an essential focus for the final chapter.

These chapters highlight significant areas of change, but they are not inclusive. Your task is to glean from the examples, images, and guidelines perspectives and tools that you can apply to other changes you encounter.

The study intends to be applicable to adults of varying ages, single or married, with or without children. If you have difficulty identifying with a particular example, perhaps another illustration will be more personally relevant for you. Use the cases as opportunities to broaden your horizons. For example, if you have no children and the chapter describes issues for parents, view the discussion as an opportunity to be more empathetic to concerns faced by your parents or by friends.

To prepare for your journey into the murky, unstable, uncomfortable world of change, reach out and meet your fellow travelers. Pick up your partially-empty knapsack. Hopefully, by the end of your six session encounter, you will have gained new tools and perspectives for your sack, new friends who appreciate your journey, and a clearer sense of God's presence with you.

[1] From "Serenity Prayer," by Reinhold Niebuhr.

—Bonnie Messer

Bonnie J. Messer, a licensed psychologist in private practice, focuses her counseling on adults facing transitions in their life. Building on a developmental perspective, she seeks to encourage awareness and growth in all aspects of the person—emotional, social, spiritual, intellectual, and physical. Bonnie has taught at Dakota Wesleyan University, Arapahoe Community College, Loretto Heights College, and the University of Denver. She counseled students and directed the Internship Program at the University of Denver's Counseling Center until making the transition to private practice.

Bonnie and her husband, Don, live in Englewood, Colorado. They are pleased to have their two grown children living nearby. Bonnie has a B.A. from Morningside College, an M.S.W. from Boston University, and a Ph.D. from the University of Denver.

CHAPTER ONE

UNDERSTANDING CHANGE: OPPORTUNITIES AND OBSTACLES

CHECKING IN

As part of getting acquainted, ask group members to share information about themselves and why they have chosen to be part of this group. If the group is larger than twelve members, ask persons to share the personal information in smaller groups. Share expectations for the study in the larger group.

DISCUSSION POINT

Using a large piece of paper or a chalkboard, record words or phrases that come to mind when you think about change. You can enumerate events, feelings, sayings, or whatever else comes to mind.

What is your view of change?

What image or symbol represents change for you?

How might you describe rapid changes you experience?

Who are some Bible people who struggled with changes in their life? Tell how they overcame obstacles and experienced personal or social transformation.

Checking In

For this first session, be prepared to share (1) your name; (2) brief information about who you are (for example, your work and your interests); and (3) why you have chosen to be a part of this group.

Imaging Change

Throughout this study, a variety of images related to change will be presented. You are encouraged to search for an image or symbol that has special meaning for you. The story of the lobster serves as a guiding image of change for me.

The lobster's hard shell protects it from danger. However, in order to grow and expand, the confining shell must be sloughed off. For a time the lobster is left exposed and vulnerable until a new covering grows to replace the old. People exhibit similarities to lobsters. To keep growing, we too must shed our old, protective shells. Life is scary without that familiar shell, but envisioning how the old shell pinched and stunted further growth can be a motivator for affirming change.

Alvin Toffler's book *Future Shock* underscores the roaring current of change that most of us experience on a daily basis. Describing the accelerated pace at which change is occurring, he suggests that it is like a "kaleidoscope run wild."[1]

We are bombarded by change at a multitude of levels. Picking up the daily newspaper, we can read about changes occurring economically, politically, and socially on an international, national, and local plane. Simultaneously, change is happening in our world of work, our family, and ourselves.

Christians recognize change as an inevitable dimension of living. The Bible, from Genesis to Revelation, shares many stories of religious persons and communities struggling to cope with change. With God's help and grace, persons can overcome obstacles; and God's Spirit can provide opportunities for personal and social transformation.

GROUP INTERACTION

Ask persons to find a partner and to share how they generally respond to changes in their life.

DISCUSSION POINT

Have persons discuss the questions highlighted in the main text.

Using a chalkboard or a large piece of paper, have members list some positive and some negative ways that persons might cope with change.

GROUP INTERACTION

Share with another person, or in a small group of three or four, examples of "predictable" and "unpredictable" change. Discuss changes that are most difficult for you.

DISCUSSION POINT

Name some surprising or unexpected feelings persons might have when they experience a positive change.

Responses to Change

Change can fill us with a sense of dizzying disorientation, disbelief, and denial. We may feel, *This can't be happening to me.* While there are days when all of us prefer the stance of an ostrich with its head in the sand, the reality is that if we are going to keep on living, and living fully, we are going to experience change.

How we respond to change is affected in part by our view of change. <u>Is change something to be avoided? Do we run out and welcome change with open arms? Or do we look backward with regret?</u> Not to change risks our becoming a stagnant pond with no fresh springs of water moving through us.

At times change feels like a loss of direction. What are we to do? We long for clear guidelines or a map. Some persons turn to a dogmatic religion or a dysfunctional cult to provide them with answers. Others escape through addictive drugs. Adventurers welcome the opportunity to experiment creatively with new ways of dealing with the changes around them. Change has the potential for both pain and growth. How we respond to a particular change, how traumatic it feels, depends on our attitudes, our capabilities, our past experiences, and the particular circumstances.

Generally, it is easier to cope with change that is predictable or anticipated. For example, we all know that children will mature physically and intellectually and will eventually move out of their parents' home. While we may have difficulty dealing with an "empty nest," it is not the same as experiencing the unpredictable crisis of a child's death due to an accident or illness.

Likewise, one can anticipate changing jobs or retiring in the future. We have opportunities to plan for the change of employment over time. To feel that one has some say about when and how one makes a career shift is quite different from when one experiences the unplanned loss of a job through the reorganizing or downsizing of one's company.

While being able to anticipate a change is helpful, many people are bewildered when they experience an avalanche of unexpected feelings along with a positive event. For example, a mother may be depressed after the birth of her child, or an employee may be overwhelmed and anxious after receiving a long-awaited promotion.

A major factor in how one deals with change reflects the degree to which one feels he or she has some control about what is happening. Studies show that persons who feel they

DISCUSSION POINT

What are some factors that might make a difference in how persons experience change?

have minimal control often experience increased feelings of depression, anxiety, and lowered self-esteem.

Whenever considering the impact of change in a person's life, one needs to keep in mind that all individuals deal differently with change. What feels like a major crisis to one person may be experienced as a minor bump in the road for another. We need to guard against the tendency to think there is only one right way to deal with disruption in our life or that everyone would surely feel as we feel. For example, two persons receive a promotion at work. For one, the promotion means the opportunity to return to his or her home state and family. For another, it means leaving a beloved home and special friends. Responses will not be the same.

Rating Life-Changing Events

T. H. Holmes and R. R. Rahe have extensively studied adults who have experienced multiple changes within a year's time frame. Their scale, the Social Readjustment Rating Scale (SRRS), consists of forty-three items of pleasant and unpleasant life events that can significantly affect an individual. Each event in their scale is assigned an LCU (Life Change Unit) that reflects the perceived severity and potential impact. Holmes and his colleagues predict that persons who have been exposed to stress events that add up to an LCU (Life Change Unit) score of 200 to 299 within recent months have a risk factor of about 50 percent of developing a major illness in the next two years. Persons with a score above 300 have a risk factor of 80 percent.[2]

Examples of events and assigned LCUs are listed below:

Death of spouse	100	Change in finances	38
Divorce	73	Child leaving home	29
Personal injury	53	Begin or end school	26
Marriage	50	Change in residence	20
Fired from work	47	Change eating habits	15
Retirement	45	Vacation	13
Pregnancy	40	Minor law violation	11

Note that both positive and negative events are listed. As discussed above, not all persons experience the same feelings or consequences from the same event.

WRITTEN REFLECTION

Ask persons to write in their journals or on paper. Give adequate time to write. Ask those who feel comfortable doing so to share their answers and insights.

GROUP INTERACTION

If your group has more than nine persons, form groups of three or four. Work in small groups to develop a scale of experiences that would have an impact on persons and assign LCUs. After groups have finished, have them share their ideas with other groups. Compare and contrast how groups differ in what they put on the scales and how they rated the LCUs.

DISCUSSION POINT

Have you ever experienced feelings different from what people expected that you "should" feel during a particular change or crisis in your life? Explain.

How did persons react when you did not show the expected feelings? How did you react to being expected to feel a certain way?

Written Reflection

Think of the major events in your life this past year. List them on a sheet of paper and assign LCUs. Ask yourself the following question: How stressful was this year compared to other years? Think of the most stressful year in your life and list those events and LCUs. (You may not be able to complete this task today but would prefer to bring your list back to share next session.)

Group Interaction

With others in the group, develop a scale of forty changes that you believe have a major impact on persons. Be sure to consider changes that might be more relevant for either women or men as well as those that might affect either gender equally. Assign LCUs to each event.

Coping With Change

While the literature on crises attempts to illustrate persons' responses to a crisis, it too can result in people being pegged to respond in certain ways. When they respond differently, they are seen as somehow abnormal.

An example comes from the field of grief counseling. We have learned that persons pass through a series of emotional states in the process of losing a loved one. This understanding has aided counselors and families in supporting persons going through the "grief process." However, on occasion bereaved persons complain that others will not accept how they are really feeling. There is no recognition of different timetables in how long one may grieve. One person commented that he had been "crying for years" as he watched his loved one die of cancer. When she finally died, he felt he had already cried most of his tears. Relief described what he was experiencing.

Responses to Change

With an understanding that not all change creates distress for all persons, let us proceed to examine some of the more common responses to change. While most of us are willing to admit that change does happen, we try to minimize the impact of the change. Our stance is "business as usual."

When a significant change event occurs, there is a temporary "dip" in our feelings and actions. We experience a feeling of disequilibrium. What do we do now? Usually, we react by implementing the coping mechanisms we have employed in the past. If this works, the feeling of disequilibrium passes and we go on.

What happens when our efforts are not effective? Shock and panic may result. While the person tries even harder to cope with the change, his or her assessment concludes that things are getting worse. Increased anxiety, despair, and lowered self-esteem may result. It is crucial that family, friends, or professional help be employed to seek to alleviate the downward spiral. At this point, the individual needs to add to his or her repertoire of coping skills and to gain additional perspectives to deal with these unexpected challenges.

Let us apply this model to a common life-changing event—the birth of a child. Learning she was pregnant, Lisa and Mike began making plans. They selected physicians, attended classes, purchased clothing and furniture, and read books. After the birth of their child, unanticipated changes began to occur. Lisa experienced exhaustion and sometimes felt depressed; Mike was shocked at how much time caring for the baby demanded. They made a good adjustment until the baby developed colic. Suddenly, they felt totally out of control. No book had prepared them emotionally for a baby who cried for hours. Assurance that the crying would pass in a few months was not calming.

Or consider the example of Jim who ended a significant relationship. He moved into a new townhome and began a more active social life. However, after a few months, he reported feeling a loss of trust, obsessive thinking about what his "ex" was doing, and an inability to sleep soundly. Lack of sleep and poor concentration began to impact his ability to function at work. Co-workers complained of his irritability, and friends stopped calling.

A third example involves Cynthia. With family proudly watching, Cynthia graduated from college full of dreams for the future. She approached her first job with enthusiasm. However, no matter how many hours she worked, she could not meet her quotas. Her self-esteem plummeted. Eventually Cynthia found herself searching for another job with her cash reserve dwindling. Unable to handle her expenses, she moved back in with her parents—an event unanticipated by all three of them. Getting out of bed in the morning to follow up on job leads became more difficult. College had not prepared Cynthia for this crisis.

DISCUSSION POINT

Have you experienced any of these responses to change or have your responses usually been different? Explain.

What responsibility does the church have to help persons through difficult times?

Should persons be expected to cope with difficult problems on their own and not "bother" the church or church members? Explain.

How might a church congregation help new parents?

What could a church congregation or a church group do to help someone like Jim?

How can a congregation or church group know when a person is having difficulties?

What response can church congregations make toward new graduates like Cynthia?

Can churches and church members do anything to help persons experiencing such problems as Cynthia and her parents? Explain.

WRITTEN REFLECTION

List three significant changes in your life. Which of these changes was most difficult? Why? Think of a difficult change in your life. Diagram this experience, noting dips and how you sought to cope. List external resources that helped you cope. Evaluate whether you achieved a higher level of functioning as a result of coping with such changes.

When persons experience success in developing new ways of coping with the changes in their life, they gain self-esteem and self-confidence. New understanding and an appreciation for one's abilities to handle tough situations usually results in a level of functioning higher than before the crisis occurred.

Qualities That Aid in the Change Process

The following eight qualities have been identified in persons who effectively cope with change:

1. Hopefulness. A positive affirmation of the future and our ability to manage its challenges.

2. Flexibility. The ability to consider a problem from a variety of perspectives and the willingness to incorporate new ideas, providing one with more options.

3. An integrated, realistic sense of who one is. A fairly objective appraisal of one's strengths and weaknesses, accompanied by a sense of humor.

4. A sense of timing. The ability to anticipate potential changes, to discern when to roll with the punches and when to take specific actions.

5. Willingness to take risks. Lacking guarantees, the resolution to proceed by utilizing available resources.

6. An autonomous sense of self. A sense of self resulting in more independent actions. The more persons control their own motives and talents, the less they are swayed by external expectations and controls.

7. Ability to relate warmly with others. Responding with empathy to the needs of others, as well as to one's own needs. A ready acceptance of support from others.

8. A unifying philosophy of life. A sense of purpose that is larger than ourselves.

DISCUSSION POINT

BIBLE STUDY

Discuss the question in the main text.

Ask different persons to read aloud the passages listed.

What expressions of hope during difficult times do you find in the Bible passages?

CHECKING IN

Each week ask the group to evaluate how their LIFE-SEARCH experience is going and to think of ways to improve the experience for everyone.

Have participants who wish to do so exchange phone numbers in order to support one another during the week.

Discussion

Which of these qualities seem the most important to you? What other qualities would you add?

In order to change or strengthen a part of ourselves, we need a vision of how we would like to be. What would you like to strengthen in your life? What will you need to do to begin the process? Make a personal commitment to begin this growth process this week. (Try for something realistic to accomplish in a week.) What could you use as a specific measure of this growth?

The God of Help and Hope

Our society places great value on being independent. To accept help often is regarded as a sign of weakness. What Bible passages do you find helpful regarding our need for support during crises?

Read Jeremiah 17:7-8 and Psalm 27:1-6.

Christian theologians often speak of a God of hope. Christians do not pretend all change is beneficial or good but remain confident in the faith that regardless of what happens, God's love and care are with us. I find solace in the words of Natalie Sleeth:

"There's a time for living and a time to die,
A time for laughing and a time to cry,
A time for wondering and knowing why,
But it's all in the hands of God."[3]

Supporting One Another

How can this group be supportive to one another with concerns being explored during this study? How would you like to be supported?

WORSHIP

Invite members to pray together as a group. Use this prayer or one of your own.

BEFORE NEXT TIME

Closing Prayer

Come, O come, heavenly God of hope. To you we bring our worries, our cares, our burdens. We confess that we are often filled more with despair than hope. We cry with the psalmist, "My sighing is not hidden from you. / My heart throbs, my strength fails me" (Psalm 38:9b-10a). We long for your presence. Fill us with assurance that with your help we can find direction out of the chaos in our life. Amen.

Before Next Week

If you have not finished the Written Reflections, complete them this week for your own benefit and to share next week, if you wish.

[1]From *Future Shock,* by Alvin Toffler (Bantam Books, Inc., 1970); page 10.

[2]From "The Social Readjustment Rating Scale," by T. H. Holmes and R. R. Rahe, in *Journal of Psychosomatic Research,* 11:1967; page 216.

[3]From "It's All in the Hands of God," copyright 1981 by A.M.S.I., quoted in *Adventures for the Soul: 35 Inspirational Poems and the Stories Behind Them,* by Natalie Sleeth (Hope Publishing Company, 1987); page 78.

Chapter Two

INEVITABLE CHANGES IN THE FAMILY

CHECKING IN

You may want to ask persons to share their Written Reflections if they completed them after the last session.

In small groups of three or four, have persons share information about the family in which they grew up.

DISCUSSION POINT

Can you think of an image or symbol that depicts your family?

What is your definition of a family? (You may want to record the definitions of a family on a large piece of paper or chalkboard.)

In what ways has the faith community been supportive to your family? In what ways has it fallen short of its promise?

Checking In

Share with one another about your family of origin (for example, number of children, whether you had any aunts, uncles, grandparents, or other persons who lived with you at some point, and so forth).

Images of the Family

What is your definition of a family? Has your definition changed in the past ten years? Many persons define a family as a married father and mother and children all living in the same home. However, this definition does not apply to the majority of families. We also find single parents and children, cohabiting adults with children, blended families, couples with grown children living away from home, adult couples without children, and single persons who have chosen to live together in a more communal setting, as well as older adults who live alone, with their children, or in a retirement or nursing home.

Throughout history Christians have cherished the family as fundamental to God's hope and intentions for loving relationships and the well-being of persons and society. Always the church's commitment has been to assist the family in the nurturing of children. The ritual of infant baptism, for example, includes the affirmation of the entire community of faith that they will be supportive in the raising of a child.

Since the 1960's, however, persons have been predicting the demise of the family. While the family has definitely changed, no other institution has been identified that can adequately take its place. We may need to think creatively about new supports for the family.

Can you recall times of significant change in the way various family members related to others in the family? Tell about one or more of those times.

We all begin life as part of a family. Our role and how we relate to our family varies widely over the years. From a helpless infant, to an inquisitive toddler, to an eager first grader, to a blushing or belligerent teenager, we constantly develop and change, challenging our parents to keep up with us. As young adults, we prepare for jobs or college and anticipate life outside our family home. In our adult years, we create our own autonomous households, exploring intimate relationships, examining the possibility of having children, buying a home, and so forth. As responsibilities expand, adults frequently find themselves actively involved in their church and community, as well as their family; ultimately they may need to take on caring for their parents. Clearly, families are always in flux—if we are not changing at the moment, someone else in the family is.

External Forces Impacting Families

The family is being buffeted by shifting currents in the local and global economy, national and international politics, value systems, health care, and role expectations for men and women. <u>Can you think of particular external events or viewpoints that have impacted your family?</u> Examples of such events would include the Great Depression in the 1930's, World War II, the polio epidemic, the Civil Rights Movement, the Vietnam War, threats of nuclear war, and the women's liberation movement.

DISCUSSION POINT

On a large piece of paper or chalkboard list external events and points of view impacting the family when you were a child.

How would the list be the same or different for families today?

WRITTEN REFLECTION

Ask group members to write answers to the questions in the main text and to follow the directions for identifying eventful times of coping with change and for drawing a family timeline. (You may want to provide large sheets of paper for the timelines.) Give adequate time to write and draw. When persons have finished, let those who are willing share their answers and timelines with others.

Written Reflection

What special memories do you have of your family? Identify eventful times when your family coped with significant changes. Draw your family's timeline. Note particular mile markers (for example, births, deaths, persons leaving or reentering the home, scrapes with the law, physical illnesses, external events). How did your family cope? Who led the way? What role did the church play?

GROUP INTERACTION

Share examples of rituals in your family. Can you recall memories of family holidays? What was your favorite holiday as a child? What made it so special?

DISCUSSION POINT

How do you define when an adolescent has made the transition to adulthood?

DISCUSSION POINT

How do your parents show they care?

What would you like them to do?

How do you show your adult children you care?

Give examples of ways parents can be over-involved in the lives of their adult children.

Family Rituals

In this time of rapid change many families complain of feeling fragmented and lacking roots. Traditions have been lost. Families need to be encouraged to revitalize or develop special rituals related to mealtimes, vacations, birthdays, or holidays. For example, a ritual in our family is to hold hands and to sing the "Johnny Appleseed Song" at the beginning of every meal.

Second-Stage Parenting

Many of us tend to define parenting as caring for children. As young adults spread their wings, parents may think their responsibilities are about over. They imagine years with decreased demands on their time, their emotional energy, their finances, and their physical space. For some these changes are greeted with relief, for others an "empty nest" symbolizes loss and grief.

However, reality frequently proves quite different from what was anticipated. Rather than downsizing homes, parents may receive requests to provide bed and breakfast for their returning adult children. Young adults who left home for school, work, marriage, military service, or just to "find themselves" may ask for their old room back. Frequently, they return with friends, spouses, and/or children. The "empty nest" can begin to feel quite crowded.

Offspring may return after painful romantic episodes, dissolved marriages, job difficulties, illness, accidents, or when the money runs out. While demands on parents may be intermittent, the intensity can be quite high when an adult child is in crisis. Parents feel much of the same old responsibility and concern but with little authority. The challenge facing parents is how to convey their caring and connectedness without becoming over-involved.

Zenith Henkin Gross offers the following helpful suggestions to parents for intergenerational living:[1]

1. Limit home returns to a clearly defined, short time span.

2. Develop firm rules on practical matters of everyday living. How much household help is desired? How is everyone's privacy honored?

3. Expect financial contributions to the household when the child gets a job.

GROUP INTERACTION

Which of these guidelines do you think might be appropriate or inappropriate for your family? Explain.

As a group, discuss how you might change or add to the guidelines suggested.

DISCUSSION POINT

What is your viewpoint on loaning money to adult children? on giving money?

GROUP INTERACTION

Share personal experiences with divorce, if you feel comfortable doing so.

How could family members, friends, and church members have been more supportive?

What is the most helpful advice you could give for dealing with an adult child's divorce?

4. Stick to your own way of life. (For example, Do you allow smoking? Are overnight guests welcome?)

5. Do not encourage dependence. Be sure that any guidance or help ultimately encourages independence.

The Role of Money

The role of money in parent-adult child interactions merits thoughtful examination. Money can be a source of love and assistance or a tool of control and perpetual dependence. Does the child interpret the money as a measure of the parent's love? Is it a way to continue to have some say in one's offspring's affairs? Does it become a tool to solicit gratitude? Or does it provide an opportunity to help fulfill a dream? "Why not have my heirs enjoy some of their inheritance while I am still around to experience their pleasure?" asks one father.

One means of clarifying the role of money involves asking: "What strings are attached?" Is this a gift or a loan? Who determines how it is spent? Is a contract signed? Are there specific repayment expectations? Is interest charged? What happens if a debt cannot be repaid? Will the parents' retirement plans be compromised? Are all parties in agreement about the meaning of the transaction? Sharing the fruits of one's labors with one's progeny can be fulfilling, but expectations must be clear.

Coping With Divorce

Families find coping with an offspring's divorce particularly traumatic. Aftershocks ripple throughout the family, causing feelings of pain and loss for years. Most adults report great difficulty in telling their parents about an impending divorce. Feelings of shame and guilt for having "failed" run rampant on the part of the parent and the adult child. Parents experience distress as they witness their child's pain. Depending on the relationship with their child's ex-mate, it can feel like the loss of a child. Additionally there are concerns about continuing relationships with grandchildren.

Divorce is not a one-time emergency. The effects shadow one's life for years to come. Parents may be asked to assist with child-care or to help financially. Families may need to welcome "instant grandchildren" in a new blended family or mourn the loss of grandchildren who move cross-country. Parents struggle to convey support and concern without over-reacting or risking having one's distance misinterpreted as lack of interest.

Aging Parents

▶ **DISCUSSION POINT**

Describe your beliefs about the care of aging parents.

Identify your fears about aging.

On the other side, roles change as parents become older. Aging can involve many positive changes, especially as long as physical health is maintained. However, with parents' diminished mental or physical well-being or financial constraints, adult children may find themselves more actively involved. Offspring resist acknowledging changes in their parents as much as do the parents themselves. Potential role-reversals are welcomed by no one. Aging parents dread potential dependency, deterioration, undignified decline, and devaluation.

Coping with aging can feel like "advancing into alien territory." Zenith Gross reports several interesting responses from mothers she interviewed. First, they feared being a burden to their adult children. Second, they felt that their children owed them nothing. Third, they did not fear being abandoned by their children, though some did acknowledge that their worst fear was asking for help and being rejected.[2]

Bible Study

BIBLE STUDY

Form pairs or small groups. Let pairs or small groups study one, two, or more of the Bible passages. After they have finished reading and discussing, have them report to the total group.

Read about the following biblical families. With what issues were these families struggling?

Adam and Eve and their sons, Cain and Abel (Genesis 4:1-16)

Noah and his family (Genesis 6:5-22)

Joseph sold into slavery by his brothers (Genesis 37)

Ruth who chose to live with her mother-in-law, Naomi (Ruth 1:1-18)

Mary and Joseph's engagement and the birth of Jesus (Matthew 1:18-25)

DISCUSSION POINT

What does our church presently offer?

What else could we provide?

The Church's Role

How can the church respond to the varying needs of families? Janet Fishburn encourages churches to provide opportunities for members to share what is working and what is not working.[3] We need to be able to share our pain within the church family. There need to be issue-specific groups to discuss topics facing families, such as premarital sex and drugs. Growth groups can provide ongoing forums for looking at concerns related to being a single adult, to parenting infants or teenagers, for individuals coping with aging parents, for couples desiring to enhance their communication skills. Programming should be intergenerational and open to mixed groups, not just married persons.

Too often in the past, the church has confused the idea of family with a particular model such as two parents and their children. Today we affirm a diversity of family forms. God did not will just one social structure but manifests love and care to people in a variety of patterns. Our family situations will change over the years, but love and care can be manifest in many types of responsible relationships.

A powerful Christian image portrays humanity as the family of God, underscoring that all persons are ultimately brothers and sisters. God's inclusive love binds and bonds us together at a deep spiritual level, enabling us to withstand even the most rapid revolutions within our family life.

WORSHIP

As a group, reflect on the meaning of the Scripture passage.

Pray together as a group. Use this prayer or one of your own.

Worship

In describing the church as a caring community, Paul states: "If one member suffers, all suffer together with it; if one member is honored, all rejoice together with it" (1 Corinthians 12:26).

Thou who has created us, bless our families. Grant us the courage, wisdom, and patience to be contributing family members. Help us not to be easily discouraged when we feel uncomfortable with changes in our family. Guard us against "tunnel vision," focusing only on family problems. May we apply to our families the same grace we receive from you. In Jesus' name. Amen.

---

[1] From *And You Thought It Was All Over: Mothers and Their Adult Children*, by Zenith Henkin Gross (St. Martin's Press, 1985); pages 248-50.

[2] From *And You Thought It Was All Over: Mothers and Their Adult Children*; pages 266-76.

[3] From *Confronting the Idolatry of Family*, by Janet Fishburn (Abingdon Press, 1991); pages 156-59.

CHAPTER THREE

RELATIONSHIPS: THE PULL BETWEEN INTIMACY AND ISOLATION

CHECKING IN

What is happening in your life that you want the group to know about?

Tell about an intimate relationship in your life. What makes it so special?

DISCUSSION POINT

How would you define an intimate relationship?

DISCUSSION POINT

How would you define a "differentiated" person?

Examine our tendency to want our mate to think and act "just like me."

How can we take Dowrick's suggestion and approach an intimate relationship in a state of "not knowing"? Why might this enhance the aliveness of a relationship?

Creating Intimate Relationships

This chapter shifts the focus from relationships within our family of origin to intimate relationships we create in our adult world. As adults, we yearn for meaningful attachments. Intimate relationships can provide us with a feeling of connection, of being fully alive. An intimate relationship provides us with the opportunity to mutually share our hopes and dreams, our fears and pains, our joys and sorrows. While no relationship can meet all our needs, we long for a special partner who affirms us and with whom we can experience the aliveness found in giving and receiving love.

An enduring relationship requires movement from being a fairly immature, undifferentiated person to a more mature person who has a sense of self, accepts responsibility for one's actions, and is able to tolerate the give and take of life with another distinctive human being. Less-healthy relationships struggle against the tendency for one's mate to grow and change; differences in thoughts, interests, and feelings are viewed as a threat. Not comfortable with a more unique or "differentiated" companion, partners employ blame, guilt, and manipulation to maintain a more "fused" relationship.[1]

In contrast, Stephanie Dowrick suggests we enhance the aliveness of our intimate relationship by approaching our mate in a state of "not knowing." "Otherwise you've shut your eyes to that person's constant processes of change."[2] While our past forms a significant part of our identity, our present experiences and feelings plus our future dreams compose significant parts of our constantly changing identity.

Fueled by a fear that being different will weaken the relationship, immature couples become more and more isolated, trapped in roles that no longer fit. The relationship stagnates. If either partner is uncomfortable with this arrangement, the only possibility for growth is viewed as occurring outside the relationship. Alternatively, in a more mature relationship, difference, otherness, unpredictability, and change are accepted as necessary to ensure a level of vitality and enjoyment for the persons as individuals and as a couple.

Unhealthy relationships pose a threat for vulnerable persons who equate being alone with emptiness, with feeling half-alive or emotionally starved. Fearing feelings of abandonment and anxiety, persons may settle for relationships in which they are not affirmed as unique individuals. The most dehumanizing of these connections are emotionally and physically abusive relationships in which one partner is told that he or she is nothing without the other person. Unfortunately, without a clear sense of self, such a distortion of reality is all too frequently accepted; and the abused partner stays, believing he or she has no viable options.

While divorce provides a regretfully necessary resolution to the pain encountered in a dysfunctional marriage, there is increased awareness that many marriages have redeemable qualities and love can bloom anew. A belief in the viability of long-term relationships, plus premarital and marital counseling can shore up shaky foundations.

It is erroneous to assume that in order to grow and change one must leave one's present relationship. Harville Hendrix cautions, "We have given credence to the idea that when trouble comes you should just change partners, when the truth is that the way you are living with that person must be changed. It's all backward. Rather than getting rid of the partner and keeping the problem, you should get rid of the problem so that you can keep the partner."[3]

DISCUSSION POINT

Do you agree or disagree with Hendrix's ideas? Explain.

What are some ways persons could work on "getting rid of the problem" so they can "keep the partner"?

DISCUSSION POINT

What image would you use to describe a long-term relationship? (A roller coaster? A tug of war? Or another image?)

Ponder Hendrix's image of a river journey as a metaphor for a marriage. What additional details can you imagine that might apply to the trip?

If we pick someone who is caring, self-aware, and willing to work, the relationship itself can be a vehicle for change and growth. Harville Hendrix uses the image of a raft trip on the Colorado River as a metaphor for a marriage.[4] The journey is not a vacation with a tour guide who does all the work. Rather, it is our responsibility to be prepared—to have a plan, a map, a life jacket, equipment, realistic expectations, and necessary skills to navigate the journey successfully. We should expect a few rough rapids and icy spills, as well as views of mountain peaks.

WRITTEN REFLECTION

Give persons time to answer the questions in the main text and to draw their diagrams in their journals or on paper. If persons in the group do not have partners, ask them to draw circles that show a significant relationship or friendship they have had or to draw the kind of relationship they would like to have. When persons have finished, let them share their insights and diagrams with another person.

DISCUSSION POINT

What are your beliefs about being single?

What is the church's responsibility to insure that all persons are considered persons of worth? How can the church do that?

What responsibility does a congregation have to address the loneliness of persons?

How can the church provide for some of the intimacy needs of persons?

What can the church do to provide support that communities and extended families used to provide?

Considering that persons are working longer hours and have less leisure time, what can churches do to help persons feel more connected?

Written Reflection

What is your definition of a healthy, intimate relationship?

Draw two circles. One represents you and should include all your interests, needs, strengths and weaknesses, desire for closeness and distance, family background, and so forth. The other circle represents your partner. Given your definition of intimacy, how close or overlapping are these circles?

The Potential for Isolation

While our need for intimacy is universal, the U.S. Census Bureau reports that the number of unmarried adults has nearly doubled in the past 20 years—from 37.5 million in 1970 to 74.9 million in 1994. More than half of this group has never married. Those who do marry are postponing it longer. In describing persons born between 1956 and 1965, Gail Sheehy notes that many of them are focusing on their needs for autonomy and are delaying serious commitments for at least ten years.[5]

Our view of single persons needs to change. While the use of terms like *spinster* and *old maid* is diminishing in our culture, acceptance of singleness as a permanent state moves slowly. We are still socialized to feel flawed if unmarried. It is time to recognize that many people will remain single, and we need to begin to shape our support systems, beliefs, and churches to fit the present reality.

Due to less contact with extended families and other sources of support, single and married persons potentially face lonelier lives. They work longer hours, have lengthier commutes, and enjoy less leisure time. Fewer attend church or civic activities. Bonnie Jacobson bemoans society's diminished communalism. She advocates that people turn to their community for support, instead of placing unrealistic expectations on our intimate relationships to meet all our needs.[6]

In no other aspect of life are we seeing so many dramatic shifts as in how people relate to one another. The potential for isolation is increasing. While we still are dependent on others to provide us with food, shelter, and heating supplies, our manner of accessing them has become more remote. Instead of a "home-cooked" meal, we can microwave a low-fat entree, engage in television channel-surfing, and play "Hearts" by ourselves on the computer.

Tori DeAngelis suggests that our "hermit's life style" is a blend of social trends.[7] Three changes cited are the mass exodus from rural areas to the city, the depersonalizing technology at home and at work, and the breakdown of the family through divorce and career moves. In particular, the country's social mobility is cited as a prime reason for the increased separation in our culture. We have lost our sense of connection. No longer are people introduced as "Gordon's son" or "Elaine is a member of the _____ family who live up near _____." Identities have to be reforged each time we move into a new community. New friendships need to be formed. But how do we make those connections?

Many hearken back to the "good old days" when everyone in town knew you by your first name, asked you about your business, and could chat with you about a shared community history. Urban life does not encourage that style of informal interaction. To ensure adequate contact, we must increase our skills in reaching out to others.

While we are living in a time of rapidly changing social mores, the emotional need to be cared for and to care for others has not diminished. The need to belong ranks as a primary human drive. A sense of belonging occurs through frequent personal contact with others and contact that confirms emotional concern and continuity. We need to know that someone cares about us. We hate to be excluded. Watch a group of children playing; notice how important it is to be chosen for a team. Solitary confinement represents one of the worst and inhumane forms of punishment.

University of Michigan sociologists have found the negative effects of social isolation on health comparable to such factors as cigarette smoking, obesity, and high blood pressure. Persons with low quality and quantity of social relationships die sooner.[8]

How do we "reach out and touch someone"? Certainly, a telephone call serves as a welcome reminder that someone cares and provides for a feeling of continuity. Researchers from Carnegie-Mellon University are conducting studies on the effect of the Internet on how people relate. The initial speculation was that those who used the Internet more often would be lonelier and more socially isolated. Preliminary findings demonstrate this prediction to be invalid. Persons who used the Internet frequently tended to be persons who were open to new experiences. For them E-mail was a pleasurable activity, one which provided a new channel of communication.[9]

We are witnessing dramatic societal shifts impacting how adults relate. However, personal, physical contact is essential. Whether working with tiny babies, isolated adults, or persons in nursing homes, the message is clear: Human beings become depressed and experience diminished quality of life without meaningful touch and personalized care.

Isolation is a potential problem for all persons, whether single or in a committed relationship. Flexibility, openness, and a genuine caring about others are essential to cultivate and sustain meaningful relationships.

DISCUSSION POINT

How can the church help persons grow toward an intimate relationship with God?

Intimacy With God

The idea and ideal of relationships permeates Christian thinking and writings over the centuries. The startling concept that God wants intimacy and thus created human beings leaps from the very first pages of the Bible. Our God does not exist in isolation but is ever seeking to relate to us in loving and liberating ways. God encourages and enhances our intimate, caring, human relationships.

WRITTEN REFLECTION

During the session or during the next week, contemplate the questions in the main text and write about your relationships and how they impact your personal growth.

Set goals for your relationships and personal goals for yourself.

Reflecting on My Relationships

How would I like my present relationships to change and grow?

Are there ways I am limiting or rejecting the growth of persons I love?

In what areas do I want to grow? What is keeping me from moving in that direction?

What nurtures and nourishes me emotionally?

Are there spiritual journeys I am putting off?

How does my church encourage my spiritual and emotional growth? What else could the church do?

DISCUSSION POINT

Form groups of three or four persons. Have each small group discuss one or two of the four questions.

DISCUSSION POINT

Discuss the case of Bob. How can his church reach out to him during this time of upheaval? What can the church do to reach out to Bob's children and to his ex-wife? What could individuals do that might not be possible for the church as an official group to do?

Have someone read 1 Corinthians 13 aloud. If anyone has a different version of the Bible, have him or her read the passage as well. Discuss the question in the main text.

Discussion Questions

1. Some theorists suggest that marriage made sense for persons with a life expectancy of forty to fifty years. <u>Is it possible to live with the same person for fifty years and not have a stagnant relationship?</u>

2. <u>How can one work to keep vitality in one's relationships?</u>

3. Gail Sheehy suggests that persons in the future will live three different lives with serial families or different partners. <u>What do you think?</u>

4. <u>How does our church respond to people who have never been married or who have been divorced?</u>

Case Study

Bob's wife recently ended their twenty-eight-year marriage. She felt unappreciated and frustrated that all they seemed to do was argue. Bob's whole world turned upside down. The home he had so proudly built now had to be sold. His children were upset and felt they were being asked to take sides. His ex-wife turned to friends; but Bob, used to handling problems on his own, felt terribly alone. How could he tell church friends why his wife was not with him? He felt like such a failure.

Bible Study

Originally written as instructions to the church in Corinth, 1 Corinthians 13 often is recited in marriage ceremonies. <u>How does this description of love relate to the descriptions of intimate relationships discussed in the chapter?</u>

Worship

Joyfully sing or read the following hymn.

When Love Is Found

When love is found and hope comes home,
   sing and be glad that two are one.
When love explodes and fills the sky,
   praise God and share our Maker's joy.

When love has flowered in trust and care,
   build both each day, that love may dare
to reach beyond home's warmth and light,
   to serve and strive for truth and right.

When love is tried as loved ones change,
   hold still to hope though all seems strange,
till ease returns, and love grows wise
   through listening ears and opened eyes.

When love is torn and trust betrayed,
   pray strength to love till torments fade,
till lovers keep no score of wrong,
   but hear through pain love's Easter song.[10]

Pray together this prayer or one of your own.

Creator God, enable us to grow in our relationships with you and with those we love. Grant that we may be open to the needs of others and encourage their growth as we seek to be mindful to our own needs for growth and nurture. Amen.

---

[1] From "Individuation: From Fusion to Dialogue" by Mark Karpel, in *Family Process*, 1976; page 72.

[2] From *Intimacy and Solitude*, by Stephanie Dowrick (W. W. Norton and Co., 1991); page 179.

[3] From *Keeping the Love You Find: A Guide for Singles*, by Harville Hendrix (Pocket Books, 1992); page 22.

[4] From *Keeping the Love You Find: A Guide for Singles*; page 15.

[5] From *New Passages: Mapping Your Life Across Time*, by Gail Sheehy (Random House, 1995); page 42.

[6] From *If Only You Would Listen*, by Bonnie Jacobson, quoted in *The APA Monitor*, Vol. 26, No. 9, September, 1995; page 12.

[7] From "*A Nation of Hermits: The Loss of Community*," by Tori DeAngelis, in *The APA Monitor*, Vol. 26, No. 9, September, 1995; page 1.

[8] From "*A Nation of Hermits: The Loss of Community*"; page 46.

[9] From "*A Nation of Hermits: The Loss of Community*"; page 46.

[10] From "*When love Is Found*" (verses 1-4), words by Brian Wren, in *The United Methodist Hymnal*, copyright 1989 by The United Methodist Publishing House; #643. Used by permission.

Chapter Four
VOCATIONAL CHALLENGES

CHECKING IN

Building on the last session, share with another member personal goals you are setting for your growth and the growth of your relationships.

In a small group of three or four, share your "work journey."

Checking In

As part of checking in, relate your "work journey." Briefly describe different jobs you have had and what you find most gratifying and frustrating about what you do.

GROUP INTERACTION

Ask a volunteer to play Jack. Ask a second volunteer to play a person from Jack's church. Ask "Jack" and the "church member" to role-play a conversation discussing Jack's view of his situation.

Discuss: Are there work issues that Christians need to consider that non-Christians might ignore? Explain.

Ask a second pair of volunteers to play Janet and a co-worker who is a church member. Ask this set of volunteers to role-play the issues that Janet is facing.

Discuss: What responsibility do church members have to reach out to struggling persons at work?

The Significance of Work

Work is a crucial part of our self-definition, whether we work as homemakers or employees in a company, are self-employed, or are unemployed. Our tasks potentially provide us with a sense of worth, social contacts, financial security, prestige, structure, and creative outlets for our energy. However, in this world of rapid change, the meaning of work is changing for many persons.

Remember amid vocational challenges and changes that work has always been valued by Christians, but work dare not be confused with worth. God values and loves us regardless of what work we do. Work is not prioritized in the kingdom of God. The Protestant reformer Martin Luther taught us that the lowest maid's job or peasant farmer's labor ranked equal in worth with the work done by the priest or bishop.

Consider the work journeys described below.

Jack has become bored with his sales job in a national company. Disillusioned with his company's products, he reports being tired of the "smoke and mirror show" he is required to perform. "I feel that I am selling my soul," he confides. Hired right out of college, Jack was taken under the vice president's wing. To quit would mean the loss of an important mentor.

Janet works for a firm where promotions are linked to moves. She has relocated every year for the past four years. Although Janet's job offers little challenge or meaning and she has no friends due to the frequent moves, she is reluctant to consider a job change. Her salary, bonus package, company car, and promise of a foreign assignment are strong incentives. Janet labors under the rattle of her "golden handcuffs."

DISCUSSION POINT

How do you see the world of work changing?

What has been your personal experience?

How do you feel about your future at work?

What feelings do workers have in facing the situations suggested?

What do disillusionment and lost security do to one's faith and one's relationship to God?

Disillusionment and Lost Security

The day of lifetime careers has vanished. Career counselors suggest that we should be prepared to make at least three major vocational shifts during our work journey. No longer can one expect to begin as an apprentice, work one's way up in the company, and be justly rewarded for the rest of one's life. Job security has become an illusion. Businesses downsize with little regard for loyalty or past performance. While jobs and whole departments are eliminated with the stroke of a pen, employees who maintain their jobs are frequently pressured to accept additional assignments, longer hours, increased travel, and undesired relocations.

Employees complain of feeling like dinosaurs. In a rapidly changing work world where skills seemingly become obsolete overnight, longtime employees are forced to compete with new high-tech college graduates. Stay-at-home mothers worry about job availability when they return to the job market. To maintain a competitive edge, creative skill repackaging or returning to school for additional training becomes a requisite.

Even if one does attain a desired position, the company's very existence is no longer ensured. In the past decade

* nearly 50 percent of all U.S. companies restructured

* over 80,000 firms were acquired or merged

* at least 700,000 organizations sought bankruptcy protection to continue operating

* more than 24 million jobs were lost.[1]

About the only guarantee is that there are no guarantees. Change is everywhere. If Rip Van Winkle were to wake up today and review the work scene, he would find a plethora of amazing differences. The increase in women working outside the home is dramatic. The number of married mothers working full-time with one or more preschool children at home tripled between 1961 and 1991.[2] For both men and women, the latest shift involves working out of the home. High-tech computers, E-mail, and a fax machine enable employees to communicate without stepping outside their door. Contract work with no health, retirement, or vacation benefits appeals to CEO's looking for ways to trim budgets.

In the 1960's, academics predicted future employees would enjoy four-day work weeks and extended leisure time. Today's employees report working longer hours, feeling more stressed, and enjoying fewer benefits. Simultaneously, their spending power has decreased.

Responses to Unpredictability

How does one respond to these unsettling changes in the work environment? Foremost, we need to accept the fact that nonstop change is the unavoidable reality of the day. Hanging on to what has worked in the past will not be sufficient. To effectively meet the challenges of the twenty-first century, our attitudes, beliefs, and skills will require significant adaptation.

Douglas H. Heath challenges adults to do more than adjust to the changes they encounter. He encourages an interactive adaptation whereby one creates "an optimal relation between adjusting to the demands of one's environment *and* fulfilling one's own needs and exercising one's fullest range of talents."[3] Viewed as a dynamic process, the disequilibrium experienced is affirmed as an opportunity for growth. Finding a new equilibrium can free a person for new enthusiasms and commitments. Energy can be redirected. Readjusting our values, creating a new balance between work, relationships, and our self-development can result in a more self-confident, whole person.

Gail Sheehy suggests that an early midlife crisis can be the "springboard out of the trap of premature obsolescence."[4] She advocates self-knowledge and communication skills as essential tools for survival in a world where employees are treated as disposable resources. Flexible thinking, convertible skills, and anticipatory planning all assist the person needing to make a career shift.

Futurist Marilyn Ferguson observed: "It's not so much that we're afraid of change or so in love with the old ways, but it's that place in between that we fear . . . It's like being between trapezes. It's Linus when his blanket is in the dryer. There's nothing to hold on to."[5]

DISCUSSION POINT

Think of different ways you and others respond to change at work. Which ways of responding are positive? Which are negative? What might be more effective ways of responding to change?

What beliefs and attitudes might you need to change?

How can you view change in the work world as an opportunity for growth?

How much of a risk-taker are you?

When contemplating a change, do you focus on the opportunities or the obstacles?

Focusing on the obstacles can be helpful if it provides the springboard to getting rid of the stumbling blocks. However, concentrating on the risks or problems can be immobilizing. Two frequently espoused reasons for seeking to avoid change are a reluctance to leave one's comfort zone and a fear of the consequences of failure. Anxiety increases when we assess a situation, assess our ability to deal with it, and conclude that we are inadequate to the task. Increased anxiety can result in the avoidance of taking risks. Clinging to the status quo can result in lowered self-esteem. How can we turn around this negative equation? If we can optimistically assess the possibilities and our ability to cope with the challenges, we are more apt to respond positively to the opportunity.

In *Wouldn't Take Nothing For My Journey Now*, Maya Angelou describes an African-American woman, Annie, with two toddlers who must fend for herself when her husband leaves. From meager beginnings selling home-cooked lunches to factory workers, she eventually opens her own store. Maya Angelou concludes:

"Each of us has the right and the responsibility to assess the roads which lie ahead, and those over which we have traveled, and if the future road looms ominous or unpromising, and the roads back uninviting, then we need to gather our resolve and, carrying only the necessary baggage, step off that road into another direction. If the new choice is also unpalatable, without embarrassment, we must be ready to change that as well."[6]

WRITTEN REFLECTION

In your journal or on a piece of paper, write your plan for seeking and maintaining a job. Share your plan with the group. What are features of your plan that could be helpful to others? What features of their plans would be helpful for you?

Above all else, positive coping with vocational changes requires a vision, a plan for the future. As children we are asked, "What do you want to be when you grow up?" While our understandings of career demands are limited in childhood, our dreams are bountiful. As adults, we need to reclaim the ability to dream and then draw on inner courage to make the plan come to fruition.

Frederick M. Hudson enjoins us: "As far as we know, human beings are the only creatures on earth capable of envisioning a future and then setting about to make it happen. We dream and imagine; we expect and plan; we invent and create. This is how new companies get born, poems get conceived, Olympic races get won, music gets written, and inventions get made."[7]

Frederick Hudson views life as cyclical, not linear, and urges adults to find meaning in the peaks and valleys of life. Rather than fight the changes we encounter, he suggests we recognize and learn to master the change process within our life.

DEALING WITH CHANGE

Life transitions, job losses, political surprises, and accidents are windows for learning rather than barriers to progress. He encourages us to enjoy the journeys we are on and to invest in learning, living, and leading.

Hudson employs the image of the adult life cycle as being like a river.

"Living in the 1990s feels like being on a raft floating down a commanding river. We have a small mast and sail, a rudder, and some poles. Sometimes when its calm, our journey is fairly effortless; we can moor the raft in an eddy near a meadow and camp for a while. At other times, the white waters of the river test every skill we have as we slide over rocks and rapids and swirl about in unforeseen directions."[8]

DISCUSSION POINT

What image would you use to describe your work journey?

Discerning a Plan for My Life

—How can I discern God's vision for my life?

—How effective am I at balancing work and the rest of my life?

—Do I view change as a time of loss or as an opportunity to develop unused strengths and talents?

—What beliefs do I hold about myself that decrease my self-confidence and my willingness to take risks?

—What beliefs would I like to have about myself?

—What "attitude adjustments" do I need to make?

—In anticipation of continued changes in my work environment, what steps do I need to take to ensure that I have viable skills and options?

GROUP INTERACTION

Form groups of three or four persons. Have each group select two or three questions to discuss. After groups have discussed, have someone from each group report insights to the total group.

Suggest that persons continue to reflect on these questions and to write their thoughts in their journals during the coming week.

Case Study

Paula, a high school graduate, had worked ten years for a company, directing a special project the past three years. Over a weekend, the CEO decided to wipe out the whole project. Within two weeks the total group, who had enjoyed working together, were dispersed to other parts of the company. Her colleagues were gone and so was Paula's focus. Paula complained of having lost her identity and her motivation. She

GROUP INTERACTION

Read about Paula. As a group, reflect on Paula's dilemma and her responses. What, if anything, could the church do to help Paula in her struggle?

was depressed; her "spirit had been wiped out." The whole process made no sense.

Paula did not feel she had the option of quitting. Her family depended on her income and health insurance. One child had a health problem that could result in an exclusion with a new insurance company.

How then was she to move on? "Plan A is gone, and there is no Plan B," she mourned. She had no motivation to begin working on redefining her job. Her immediate goal was to get out of the hole she felt she was in, to feel more in control. After attending a women's retreat at her church, Paula reported developing a new image of the caterpillar who needs to be in a chrysalis before becoming a butterfly. Recognizing the need for a time of transition helped validate her need to "just be" for a while.

How do you feel about sharing struggles with your work situation with persons in your congregation? Is it appropriate to share struggles such as Paula is facing with others in the congregation, or should church members just keep those things to themselves? Explain.

Who Am I As a Worker?

List your work experiences.

List three particular successes.

What are your strengths and weaknesses?

What qualities of yourself would you like to include more in your work experiences?

What jobs might you like to explore in the future?

Who could you talk to about job possibilities?

What would be obstacles to your making a vocational change?

WRITTEN REFLECTION

On paper or in your journal, answer the questions that seek to define you as a worker. When you have finished, share your insights with a partner.

The Impact of Values on Our Work

What we value influences our choice of jobs. List ten values that are important to you in your work, for example, salary, benefits, location, flexibility, hours, vacations, co-workers, adventure, personal satisfaction, challenge, creativity, security, variety, freedom to be yourself, helping people, work environment, friendliness, prestige, and leadership opportunities.

Prioritize your list, noting the four values that are most

GROUP INTERACTION

Follow the instructions in this section. Then share your top four values with another group member. Can you agree on four values important to both of you? Report these four values to the larger group.

important. Share your values and priorities with another group member. Discuss why these four values are particularly important to you.

BIBLE STUDY

Do you feel that you earn love from God and others through working? How can you separate the feelings you gain from work from your relationship with God?

Bible Study

We do not earn God's love and grace like we earn a paycheck or win an award. The Christian doctrine of justification by grace alone emphasizes that God's enduring love for us exists whether we are employed or unemployed, successful or unsuccessful, rich or poor, famous or unknown. Read Galatians 2:16.

Discuss the turmoil expressed by the author of Psalm 38:8-22. How do we turn to God in times of despair when feelings of hopelessness run rampant?

WORSHIP

Pray the prayer written by Reinhold Niebuhr. Place special emphasis on "courage to change the things I can."

Prayer

God, grant me the serenity to accept the things I cannot change; courage to change the things I can; and wisdom to know the difference. Living one day at a time; enjoying one moment at a time; accepting hardship as the pathway to peace. Taking, as He did, this sinful world as it is, not as I would have it. Trusting that He will make all things right if I surrender to His will. That I may be reasonably happy in this life, and supremely happy with Him forever in the next.[9] Amen.

[1]From *Adapting to Change*, by Carol Kinsey Goman (Crisp Publications, Inc., 1992); page 3.

[2]From *New Passages: Mapping Your Life Across Time*, by Gail Sheehy (Random House, Inc., 1995); page 42.

[3]From "Wanted: A Comprehensive Model of Healthy Development," by Douglas H. Heath in *The Personnel and Guidance Journal*, January, 1980; page 396.

[4]From *New Passages: Mapping Your Life Across Time*; page 78.

[5]From Marilyn Ferguson quoted in *Adapting to Change*; page 1.

[6]From *Wouldn't Take Nothing For My Journey Now*, by Maya Angelou (Random House, 1993); page 24.

[7]From *The Adult Years*, by Frederick M. Hudson (Jossey-Bass, Inc., 1991); page 74.

[8]From *The Adult Years*; page 51.

[9]From *"Serenity Prayer,"* by Reinhold Niebuhr.

CHAPTER FIVE

RELOCATION OR DISLOCATION?

CHECKING IN

What is happening in the lives of the group members that they want to share with the group?

Have the group members answer the questions in the main text. Then, as a group, share words and feelings that come to mind when talking about moving.

BIBLE STUDY

Can you think of other Bible people who faced moving and dislocation?

Do you identify with any of the Bible people who moved? Explain.

Checking In

Think back over the moves in your life. <u>How many times have you moved? What is your general response to moving?</u> Share with the group a move that was particularly memorable for you

Bible People Moved

Many Biblical images relate to moving. Early in the Hebrew Bible, Adam and Eve were forced out of the garden of Eden. Noah and his family sought shelter in a boat when their land became flooded. Lot's wife stopped to look back at her home and was turned into a pillar of salt. Moses and the Israelites fled from Egypt and wandered for years in the wilderness before entering the Promised Land. After the death of her husband, Ruth told her mother-in-law Naomi, "Where you go, I will go." A familiar New Testament image is that of Mary, Joseph, and their infant son seeking a safer life in Egypt.

Read Genesis 12:1-9. At the age of seventy-five, Abram (Abraham) followed God's command and moved his household and the household of his nephew to the land of Canaan. When Abram arrived, he built an altar to God. When he moved on, he built another altar and worshiped. <u>What kind of faith might it have taken for Abram to move when God told him to go? Have you ever felt that God was leading you to move? When you arrive at your destination after a move, how do you recognize and celebrate that God is still with you?</u>

On the Move Today

Moving is not a new phenomenon for persons around the world. War and famine frequently result in mass migrations. In the United States approximately one in five Americans moves every year. One-half of these moves are job-related. It has been suggested that the middle-class professional is the new migrant worker.

DISCUSSION POINT

What could you pack in your "suitcase" to assist you during a move?

The suggested guiding image for this chapter is a suitcase. What do you need to pack in your suitcase to help you with this relocation? What fond memories, acquired treasures, necessities need to be included? What garbage can be discarded?

For years we have lived with the myth that most persons moved with relative ease and little anxiety or discomfort. Many persons struggling with a move felt hesitant to share these feelings with others, assuming that they were the only ones who struggled. Persons who are forced to move (like Adam and Eve) are particularly reticent to share their stories. Lot's wife provides a chilling metaphor of what can happen to a person who looks back. Persons are encouraged to maintain "a stiff upper lip" and to move forward. Why should a spouse or children be upset with a transfer that will result in a "nicer" house and greater financial benefits? How could a person who had achieved a promotion be in mourning?

DISCUSSION POINT

How does it feel to have someone recognize your feelings?

What resources do you know of that can help persons facing a move?

How can you let your real feelings about a move be known when you think you "should" have other, more acceptable feelings?

What does our church offer to persons who have recently moved?

How does our congregation help persons form new relationships and find help for special needs?

What more could our church be doing to help in these areas?

Lone voices in the wilderness have begun to be heard and have been met with a mixture of relief, concern, and support. While recognizing that moves have many positive possibilities, new writings are also documenting that moves can be accompanied by feelings of sadness, loneliness, depression, anger, disorientation, and anxiety. For example, Audrey T. McCollum, in *The Trauma of Moving: Psychological Issues for Women*, points to the myriad of adjustments challenging one in the process of a move.[1]

We need to be more sensitive to the particular difficulties experienced by the "trailing spouse," such as loss of status related to one's professional position, demotions, and lowered career goals. Churches have begun to offer support groups for persons who have recently moved, recognizing that one does not quickly build new friendships or know where to turn to get help for special needs.

DISCUSSION POINT

How do you respond to a move?

What can you do for a support system after a move?

Reactions to Moving

Three months after a recent move, a newcomer reported that although the boxes were unpacked and pictures were on the walls, something was missing. Upon further consideration, he concluded that what was lost were his friends and familiar surroundings. His support system was missing. His relocation had resulted in feelings of dislocation.

When anticipating a move, one needs to be mindful that a person can experience a variety of reactions. It can feel particularly confusing when one is having positive and negative reactions at the same time, yet that is frequently the human experience. Additionally, not all members of the same family will encounter the same feelings, nor necessarily respond in the same time frame.

A move may have many positive responses. A friend commented that she "thrives on novelty." She reacts to a move with excitement. A move offers her new challenges and opportunities to meet new people. For others, there is the recognition of "work well-done" and a feeling of being ready to move on. Relocation frequently is the result of a promotion and thus involves enhanced status. For others, the move can provide the occasion to relocate to a more desirable part of the country or to be nearer family.

For many, however, there also tends to be some feelings of sadness and depression. Familiar places, activities, friends, and family are no longer readily available. It is particularly difficult if a family member feels it is unacceptable to speak of one's feelings of distress or anger.

The person taking the new job may feel restrained in admitting such doubts. The extended family is mourning their loss. How can the person who made the decision to move feel free to share feelings? The family has been uprooted and is in disarray because of these decisions. What about the trailing spouse? Frequently the spouse feels it would be disloyal to speak of misgivings when one's mate appears to be so excited about the new opportunities. When one cannot share feelings with anyone, feelings of aloneness increase.

Relocated in an unfamiliar community, persons may experience loneliness and vulnerability. Whom does one talk to? Stripped of one's usual means of relating, one can easily feel outside the mainstream of community activities. In negotiating a new environment, one seeks to tolerate "not knowing." However, "not knowing" becomes less tolerable when one has a sick child or the furnace quits working.

DISCUSSION POINT

How can you take care of yourself and your needs first so that you can better take care of those who depend on you?

What are the "little details" that you would miss if you moved from your present location?

In preparing for a move, many parents tend to focus on the needs of their children. Specific attention is placed on enrolling the children in schools that complement special interests or needs. But what about the needs of the adults? Grownups also lose friends, family members, and special activities that add meaning to life. I am frequently reminded of the recommendation on airlines: "In case of an emergency, first put on your own oxygen mask, then assist those who are dependent on you."

Adults frequently overlook the importance of little details in their daily activities that make life more enjoyable. We take for granted that friendly wave to the neighbor when bringing in the newspaper, greeting a friend at the grocery store, the chat with one's barber or hairdresser, the kid down the block who will help clean the sidewalk or play ball with your son or daughter, or that special deli that makes your favorite dessert. With a move, one is suddenly thrown into a new environment in which you know nothing about schools, doctors, bakeries, churches, or where to go for a hug on a bad day.

Due to the loss of a significant part of one's support system, persons may find that they are increasingly dependent on their partner. Unfamiliar, increased dependency can be uncomfortable for everyone. How can ambivalent feelings be expressed when the only person available to listen is the person on whom one is so dependent?

Trailing partners frequently speak of feelings of helplessness, of lack of control. Persons also may share a feeling of loss of identity. Customary sources of recognition are not readily available. Giving up a meaningful job and colleagues is difficult. Mates frequently report having to start over or to accept lateral positions. Having to lower career goals can result in decreased self-esteem. The "human spirit does not take easily to diminution or anonymity once it has known better things."[2]

Society has not encouraged the expression of feelings regarding losses. While positive thinking is important, permission to acknowledge the whole range of one's feelings is essential if one is going to muster all one's coping resources. Minimizing one's stress makes it difficult to develop helpful strategies. In order for a person to cope with stressors related to moving, it is important that the person is able to maintain a sense of identity and competence. Persons need to feel that they are supported and that they have some say in the process.

GROUP INTERACTION

Study the five guidelines offered in the text. Give an example of how you have implemented one of these guidelines. What additional guidelines would you offer to assist persons coping with a move?

Guidelines for Adjusting to a Move

What can one do to ease some of the stress of moving? Above all else, recognize that a move is stressful, even when one is looking forward to the change. The following guidelines are suggested for helping one cope with a move.

First, when anticipating a move, persons need to be *actively involved* in the process. A negative response to a move is more likely when a person feels one has no say—no sense of control over one's own destiny. Whether you are the employee, the mate, or another family member, the gains and losses for all affected by the move need to be explored.

Second, *learn as much as you can about the new community* before you arrive. Visit the community, if possible, thus having an opportunity to get a visual image of the locale and to meet community members. Housing, job opportunities, special services, and schooling for family members can be explored. The goal is to eliminate as much mystery or uncertainty as possible.

Third, *acknowledge your feelings*. One needs to feel free to express all one's emotions—to rejoice, to mourn, to be angry, and to admit being overwhelmed. Too often we try to hide our feelings. Pulling back and not sharing with others can result in feelings of isolation and estrangement. One woman with tears streaking down her face whispered, "I have no right to be unhappy. I have everything—my husband is successful, the house is beautiful. What's wrong with me?" The more she turned the blame inward, the more depressed she became. If feelings cannot be expressed, energies are put into keeping concerns quiet, rather than being available to mobilize one's resources.

Fourth, before and immediately after the move takes place, one can begin to *purposefully seek new support systems*. Some companies are now providing in-house counselors to offer assistance to all family members. Realtors in major cities have begun to employ "relocation specialists" to help ease transitions. A dilemma reported by some is that residents in the new neighborhood are hesitant to invest in developing significant ties if they anticipate that the newcomer may move again within a year or two. Such reactions require more intention in reaching out and developing friendships in the larger community.

Active membership in a community of faith can aid the transition from one location to another. Singing favorite hymns, reciting familiar prayers, and connecting with the family of

God in a new place helps alleviate the pain of dislocation and provides new beginnings, pregnant with positive possibilities for growth through change. Many churches offer support groups for newcomers, providing practical information on doctors, baby sitters, lawn services, and much more, as well as lending an ear to hear and normalize the range of feelings experienced.

Fifth, *expect your "moving in" to take time.* Many people report that it takes at least two years before they feel really settled. Also recognize that other family members will deal with this transition in their own way and on their own time schedule. Being sensitive to others' varying time cycles can ease the tension of feeling out-of-step with everyone else.

One cannot relocate without a period of dislocation. The goal is to recognize that moving does involve upheaval and to seek to diminish the pain and stress as much as possible while affirming the necessary steps in our journey through life.

DISCUSSION POINT

Discussion

Recall your most difficult move. What made it so problematic?

Recall your best move. What facilitated that process?

What could our church do to assist persons who are in the process of leaving or moving into our community?

GROUP INTERACTION

Read the case study of Jason. As a group, name Jason's many feelings. Can you identify with any of his concerns? Explain.

Case Study

Jason came in for counseling after a fight with his bride of eight months. He reported feeling depressed and stated that he was seriously questioning his decision to take a promotion and move to a new city. Further complicating matters, his wife had taken a demotion to make the move. How could Jason now admit he had made a mistake?

Out of guilt related to asking his wife to move, Jason agreed to buy a house he disliked. He missed the familiarity of their old neighborhood and friends. Jason described spending a frustrating Saturday evening driving from one shopping center to another hunting for a particular ethnic food they both enjoyed. They both felt so unsupported. Nothing was working right. He felt a bit like Moses in the wilderness.

BIBLE STUDY

Read the passages from the Psalms. What feelings are expressed? Share your understanding of these Scriptures with the group.

What Scriptures do you find comforting when feeling as if you are in an "alien land"?

WORSHIP

Close the session with the printed prayer or one of your own.

Bible Study

In both relocation and dislocation, a person can sense some spiritual lows in the drama and trauma of moving. Sometimes remembering some basic Christian assurances, such as Jesus promising "I am with you always," can provide a comforting or uplifting perspective during a difficult day. Christian faith contends we are never abandoned because God's grace is with us wherever we are or whatever changes occur.

Read the lament of Psalm 137:1-7 over the loss of the Jewish homeland and the thanksgiving in Psalm 68:4-10 as the psalmist feels God's presence in a new land.

Closing Prayer

Guardian, Guide, I have no pillar of cloud by day nor fire by night. Yet I sense your presence with me, God of the journey. Walk with me into new and unknown lands. Encircle my trembling heart with your peace. Give me the courage to face what is before me. Fill me with sensitivity and strength that I may be aware of and honor the dislocating feelings and needs that accompany a relocation. Amen.

[1]*The Trauma of Moving: Psychological Issues for Women*, by Audrey T. McCollum (Sage Library of Social Research, 1990); page 182.

[2]From *"The Effects of Relocation on the Trailing Spouse,"* by Marjorie Bayes (Smith College Studies in Social Work, Vol. 59, No. 3, June, 1989).

Chapter Six
CARING FOR YOURSELF DURING TIMES OF CHANGE

CHECKING IN

Ask persons to share how they have been dealing with change. What has been happening in their life that they would like the group to know about? Then ask them to share a strategy they use to comfort themselves.

DISCUSSION POINT

How do you feel about caring for yourself?

Do you feel caring for yourself is selfish? Explain.

Why is it important to love oneself?

Checking In

How have you been dealing with change in your life?

What has been happening in your life that you would like the group to know about?

Share a strategy you employ to comfort yourself when feeling distressed and confused.

Perspectives on Self-Care

Many Christians resist admonitions to take care of themselves. "It feels so selfish," they explain. *The World Book Dictionary* defines *selfish* as (1) "caring too much for oneself and too little for others" and (2) "showing care solely or chiefly for oneself."[1] In an attempt not to be selfish, persons frequently move to the opposite extreme—selflessness. The dictionary defines *selfless* as "having no regard or thought for self."[2] I am advocating a position that balances the needs of others and of oneself. Caring should not be an either/or proposition but should focus on the needs of all involved. Christian teachings warn against selfishness and self-centeredness, labeling them as sin; but the church does not oppose a healthy love of self.

We receive instructions from the Great Commandment: "You shall love the Lord your God with all your heart, and with all your soul, and with all your strength, and with all your mind; and your neighbor as yourself" (Luke 10:27). We are to love our God, our neighbors, *and* ourself. In fact, many times if we do not care for ourself, we can be of little help to others. This final chapter focuses on caring for ourselves while changes swirl about us.

DISCUSSION POINT

What images do you have of caring for yourself during times of change? Explain.

Tell about a time when you or someone you know reacted to change like Alice did.

Tell about a time when you or someone you know reacted to change like a person who is remodeling.

How can you create a temporary shelter for yourself during times of upheaval? What are some things you would need? What additional things would you like to have in your temporary shelter?

DISCUSSION POINT

Tell about a time you denied that change was affecting your life. What happened as a result of the denial?

Can denial ever serve a useful purpose during change? Explain.

Images of Change

Two images come to mind as I envision how we care for ourself during a time of tumultuous change. The first is of Alice who tumbles down a rabbit hole into a strange wonderland. Intrigued and determined to find a way to change herself to fit through a tiny doorway, Alice precedes to drink from unknown bottles and nibble on small cakes that change her size unpredictably. With little planning or forethought or concern for maintaining her sense of well-being, Alice stumbles on through a variety of misadventures. Upon meeting the Caterpillar, who asks her who she is, Alice confesses, "I—I hardly know, sir, just at present—at least I know who I was when I got up this morning, but I think I must have been changed several times since then."[3] Like Alice, many of us plunge ahead with little vision of where we are going; and, like Alice, we encounter some very odd and frightening incidents.

In contrast, the second image portrays a person who plans to remodel or change one's home. Rather than just beginning, one engages in preplanning to discern the unique qualities deserving preservation, as well as identifying features requiring updating. From this early visioning, one proceeds to draw up specific blueprints, employ a contractor to implement the plans, and create a temporary shelter in which to live while implementing the changes.

This final chapter focuses on the process of developing a safe "temporary shelter" that honors who we are and what we need during a time of upheaval. Needless to say, some changes cannot be preplanned; however, the need to stop and create a safe holding environment remains relevant.

Guidelines for Care of Oneself

1. Acknowledge the change.
   In order to take adequate care of oneself, one begins by acknowledging that something unusual is taking place and that special action is required. Denial interferes with our ability to take appropriate steps. For example, the person who denies a physical ailment deprives himself or herself of medical consultation that might eliminate the problem or could prevent further decline.

GROUP INTERACTION

Give each person a sheet of paper and a pen or pencil. Ask the group members to list changes that persons might face sometime in their life. Next to each change, have them put how long they think it might take to adjust to such a change. When all have finished their list, talk about the length of time they think sample changes might take. Discuss the following questions: Why do different persons have the same or different ideas about how much time it might take to adjust to particular changes? What might make the difference in the length of time it takes different persons to adjust?

DISCUSSION POINT

Think of a time family and friends helped you through a difficult experience of change. What was the change, and what did persons do that was helpful?

What were some unhelpful actions that persons performed with the intention of being helpful?

What might be done to insure that friends and family who really want to help do so in ways that will be helpful rather than unhelpful?

2. Take the time.
   Upon acknowledging change, allow adequate time to provide for necessary transformations. Used to living our life on the fast track, we frequently feel pressured to make quick decisions in reaction to a change. Slow down, be reflective; this is the only life you have the opportunity to live.

William Bridges (*Managing Transitions.* Addison-Wesley Publishing Company, 1993) refers to this period as the time of "transition." The previous phase must be completed before attempting to begin a new facet of our life. A time of transition allows us the opportunity to say our goodbyes, mourn our losses, or celebrate our victories and then begin to plan for the future.

Persons dealing with a major change, such as the loss of a mate, are encouraged not to change locations or to make other major shifts for two years. One does not need to wait two years to make many decisions, but give yourself permission to take whatever time you need.

Tim, who recently experienced major upheaval, described feeling like a grapevine. At present he is in a dormant stage, but he knows there will be a time of new beginnings in the future; and he is beginning to gain a vision of what he wants that life to be like.

3. Enlist the help of family and friends.
   When you are heavy-burdened, surround yourself with people who are understanding and supportive. Be willing to draw support from family, friends, fellow church members, and colleagues who are willing to be attentive listeners and who will seek to understand the significance of what is happening to you.

Caring persons can be unsure as to how to comfort you. You may need to teach them what would be most helpful for you. Ruth, whose husband was slowly dying from an incurable disease, explained to her well-meaning friends that she did not need to sit around and talk about her husband's illness. She needed breaks away from the sadness, opportunities to talk about more hopeful things. To laugh and be silly made it possible for her to go back and deal with the stark realities of the changes that were occurring for her and her husband.

How do you feel about seeking professional help to cope with change?

In addition to pastors and counselors, what other kinds of professionals are available to help persons cope with change?

Name some sources of continuity that have provided stability for you through a time of change.

What relaxes and nurtures you during times of change?

What do you think of the idea of "imaging"—or creating a mental image of—a safe place during times of stress?

Have you ever tried such imaging? Tell about your experience.

Can you think of other unhealthy beliefs?

Which have been detrimental to you as you faced change?

What healthy beliefs can help you through times of change?

4. Seek professional help.
   At times the support and understanding of those with whom we regularly interact is just not enough. Contacting your pastor or a counselor who can help you sort out what is taking place, your feelings about these events, and how you want to respond can help to ease the confusion and burden. Rather than being interpreted as a sign of weakness when a person seeks help, counselors view reaching out for assistance as a sign of strength and motivation. In a society that places so much importance on self-reliance, seeking guidance from others is truly an act of courage.

5. Sort out what is changing and what is continuing.
   While one may feel overwhelmed by the enormity of the changes occurring, not everything is ending. What is continuing in your personal life? your work? your community? Identify sources of continuity within yourself and within your external world. These areas of sameness can provide an anchor—a source of stability when it feels we have lost our rudder.

6. Make time to play.
   When dealing with significant changes, one also needs time to play. Whether this means taking a vacation, visiting a friend, signing up for an art class, joining the church choir, renewing interest in a sport, curling up in front of the fireplace more often, or going for walks, do something special and playful that is nurturing for you. Anne Morrow Lindberg's book *Gift From the Sea* provides a potent model of a busy woman who made time to meditate and write, thus nurturing herself along with her family.

7. Image a safe place.
   We need to consciously create a shelter from the storm. When craving space to gain perspective, it is helpful to image a haven. Some persons image their parents' kitchen, their church's sanctuary, a warm spot on the beach, or a quiet hideaway in the mountains—a place where one can rest and feel safe. After a hurricane, one must seek temporary shelter until one's home is rebuilt. When you experience chaos, do you have a "safe place"?

8. Beware of harmful beliefs.
   Especially with unwelcome changes, one tends to ask, "Why me? What have I done to deserve this upheaval?" There can be a belief that one is being punished. In the Bible, Job stands out as a righteous man to whom all manner of bad things happened. His flocks and herds were destroyed; all his children perished under a collapsed house; his body was covered with "loathsome sores." What

had Job done to deserve this? Ultimately, Harold S. Kushner suggests, we need to move beyond the question of "Why did this happen to me?" to "Now that this has happened, what shall I do about it?"[4]

Another unhelpful response occurs when one minimizes one's own difficulties because others have greater problems. "I feel so guilty when I complain about losing my job," sighed Laura. "At least I have no children to worry about feeding, and no one is dying." True, "it could be worse," and it is helpful to recognize that not everything is bad in one's life. But there are times when one needs to stop, realize what has been disrupted in one's life, and mourn one's losses. I am not advocating becoming a life-long martyr, but it is important to acknowledge the significance of the changes encountered.

Another common belief that serves as a stumbling block in our journey postulates that "life is fair." We operate under the assumption that the most deserving person gets the promotion, the most caring person lives a longer life, the most devoted parent raises the most appreciative children. Yet we know that suffering is not evenly distributed. We harbor unrealistic expectations of life. Life is not fair. Sitting around waiting for justice to reign, smoldering in our bitterness and anger, will not enable us to begin to rebuild.

How might developing a vision help lead you out of the chaos and confusion that can accompany change?

9. Develop a vision.

    It is hard to move forward without a plan. Frederick Hudson suggests that many of us "back into the future with less and less sense of direction."[5] Sometimes we need a new, updated map; but of paramount importance is a vision. Many of us fear a Humpty-Dumpty future: We will fall off our wall, and no one will be able to put us back together again. In contrast, Joyce Rupp suggests, "even a perfect egg must break for a new life to begin."[6] We need a vision of a new beginning that builds on our strengths but that will offer us new horizons. It takes real courage to pick oneself up and to begin to dream new dreams.

How can finding time for God help you with the changes in your life?

10. Set aside time for prayer and meditation.

    Beware of rushing around like Alice. Take time to be in communion with God. Seek to discern the meaning of these changes in your life, and enlist the help of God in gathering the strength to face what has happened as well as the future. In *Praying Our Goodbyes,* Joyce Rupp reminds us that the parting expression *goodbye* (originally "God-be-with-ye" or "Go-with-God") was used as a recognition that God was a significant part of our journey.[7] There is comfort in recognizing the presence of God; we are not alone.

WRITTEN REFLECTION

Give group members an opportunity to write, using the questions and directions in this section as a guide. Let persons share their thoughts with at least one or two other persons, if not with the whole group.

How can other group members support them in their commitments?

Encourage group members to use the list as a challenge for committing to implement specific changes in their life.

Opportunities for Renewal

Use this list as a challenge for making a commitment to implement specific changes in your life. Begin a Written Reflection during the session using the following questions and directions. Share your ideas with others during the session. These ideas, however, take more reflection than you can do during a LIFESEARCH session. Continue to use this list after the study to write additional thoughts and to make positive changes in your life.

—What are your dreams?

—What obstacles block you from pursuing your dreams?

—Set some new goals for yourself. What would you like to try before you die?

—How can you be more of an active participant in your life and less an observer?

—Are there enjoyable things you used to do that have slipped out of your life?

—How can you find value in what you are going through and learn from this experience?

—Integrate more fun into your life.

—Start a journal to help you get in touch with your feelings and visions for your life.

—Challenge yourself to do something you thought you could not do. Beware of living life so safely that you do not feel alive.

—Identify personal, unhelpful beliefs that have the potential for sabotaging your efforts.

BIBLE STUDY

Do you have outdated, negative, or inaccurate beliefs that need to be eliminated or updated?

Are there healthy actions or beliefs you have lost or abandoned over the years that need to be reinstated?

What new beliefs or perspectives would you like to claim as part of your adult identity?

Bible Study

This chapter encourages persons to learn new ways to cope with problems, to get rid of childlike, simplistic beliefs. In 1 Corinthians 13:11, Paul reflects this changing perspective: "When I was a child, I spoke like a child, I thought like a child, I reasoned like a child; when I became an adult, I put an end to childish ways."

WORSHIP

Encourage members to meditate briefly about the struggles of others in the group, as well as their own struggles.

Form a circle and pray Joyce Rupp's prayer.

Close by going around the circle and bidding one another, "God be with you" or "Go with God."

Closing Worship

Let us join in Joyce Rupp's prayer:

"God of Exodus, I am off on an inner road never traveled before. Deep within, where only your eyes see, there is so much mystery, greyness, restlessness. I want so much to have a sense of direction, to know where I am and where I ought to be headed. But the dark and the questions stay. You ask me to be full of faith, to believe deep within that you are my signpost, that you are my wisdom and my guide, and to trust in your presence. Your words to me are clear: 'Do not fear. I go before you.'

"But the winter of my spirit wears on. The days pass by. I plod along like boots too big on a small child. Only, I do not marvel like the young one, or pause to wonder at the beauty. Instead, I just trudge and forge ahead, no spark of love, no charge of joy, no spiritual energy . . . .God of my depths, I cry out to you to be my guide. Help me to have a strong sense of inner direction and grant that I may have the reassurance of knowing that I am on the right path. Take all that is lost in me and bring it home to you."[8] Amen.

[1]From *World Book Dictionary* (selfish)

[2]From *World Book Dictionary* (selflessness)

[3]*Alice's Adventures in Wonderland,* by Lewis Carroll (Penguin Books, first published in 1865); page 54.

[4]From *When Bad Things Happen to Good People,* by Harold S. Kushner (Avon Books, 1981); page 136.

[5]From *The Adult Years: Mastering the Art of Self-Renewal,* by Frederick M. Hudson (Jossey-Bass Publishers, 1991); page 22.

[6]From *Praying Our Goodbyes,* by Joyce Rupp (Ave Maria Press, 1988); page 44.

[7]From *Praying Our Goodbyes,* page 17.

[8]From *Praying Our Goodbyes,* pages 139-40.

THE LifeSearch GROUP EXPERIENCE

Every LifeSearch group will be different. Because your group is made up of unique individuals, your group's experience will also be unique. No other LifeSearch group will duplicate the dynamics, feelings, and adventures your group will encounter.

And yet as we planned LifeSearch, we had a certain vision in mind about what we hoped might happen as people came together to use a LifeSearch book for discussion and support around a common concern. Each LifeSearch book focuses on some life concern of adults within a Christian context over a six-session course. LifeSearch books have been designed to be easy to lead, to encourage group nurture, and to be biblically based and needs-oriented.

Each chapter in this LifeSearch book has been designed for use during a one and one-half hour group session. In each LifeSearch book, you will find
• times for group members to "check in" with each other concerning what has gone on in their lives during the past week and what they wish to share from the past week concerning the material covered in the group sessions;
• times for group members to "check in" about how they are doing as a group;
• substantial information/reflection/discussion segments, often utilizing methods such as case studies and simulation;
• Bible study segments;
• segments in which a specific skill or process is introduced, tried out, and/or suggested for use during the week to come;
• segments that help group participants practice supporting one another with the concerns being explored.

LifeSearch was not planned with the usual one hour Sunday school class in mind. If you intend to use LifeSearch with a Sunday school class, you will need to adapt it to the length of time you have available. Either plan to take more than one week to discuss each chapter or be less ambitious with what you aim to accomplish in a session's time.

LifeSearch was also not planned to be used in a therapy group, a sensitivity group, or an encounter group.

> A LifeSearch group is simply a group of persons who come together to struggle together from a Christian perspective with a common life concern.

No one is expected to be an expert on the topic. No one is expected to offer psychological insights into what is going on. However, we do hope that LifeSearch group members will offer one another support and Christian love.

We will count LifeSearch as successful if you find your way to thought-provoking discussions centered around information, insights, and helps providing aid for living everyday life as Christians.

You might find it helpful to see what we envisioned a sample LifeSearch group might experience. Keep in mind, however, that your experience might be quite different. Leave room for your creativity and uniqueness. Remain receptive to God's Spirit.

Dealing With Change

 You sit in the living room of a friend from church for the second session of your LIFESEARCH group. Besides you and your host, four other persons are present, sitting on the sofa and overstuffed chairs. You, your host, your group leader, and one other are church members, although not all of you make it to church that regularly. The remaining two persons are neighbors of the leader. You chat while a light refreshment and beverage are served by the host.

 Your leader offers a brief prayer and then asks each of you to share what has been going on in your lives during the past week since you last met. One member shares about a spouse who had outpatient surgery. Several mention how hectic the week was with the usual work- and family-related demands. Prayer concerns and requests are noted.

 This session begins with a written reflection. The leader draws your attention to a brief question in the beginning of the chapter you were assigned to read for today. Group members are asked to think about the question and to write a short response.

 While the leader records responses on a small chalkboard brought for that purpose, members take turns sharing something from their written reflections. A brief discussion follows when one group member mentions something she had never noticed before.

 Group members respond as the leader asks for any reports concerning trying out the new life skill learned in the previous session. Chuckles, words of encouragement, and suggestions for developing the new skill further pepper the reports.

 The leader notes one of the statements made in the assigned chapter from the LIFESEARCH book and asks to what extent the statement is true to the experience of the group members. Not much discussion happens on this point, since everyone agrees the statement is true. But one of the members presses on to the next statement in the LIFESEARCH book, and all sorts of conversation erupts! All six group members have their hot buttons pushed.

 Your leader calls the group to move on to Bible study time. You read over the text and then participate in a dramatic reading in which everyone has a part. During the discussion that follows the reading, you share some insights that strike you for the first time because you identify with the person whose role you read.

 You and the other group members take turns simulating a simple technique suggested in the book for dealing with a specific concern. Everyone coaches everyone else; and what could have been an anxiety-producing experience had you remained so self-conscious, quickly becomes both fun and helpful. You and one of the other group members agree to phone each other during the week to find out how you are doing with practicing this technique in real life.

 It's a few minutes later than the agreed upon time to end, but no one seems to mind. You read together a prayer printed at the end of this week's chapter.

 On the way out to your car, you ponder how quickly the evening has passed. You feel good about what you've learned and about deepening some new friendships. You look forward to the next time your LIFESEARCH group meets.

This has been only one model of how a LIFESEARCH group session might turn out. Yours will be different. But as you give it a chance, you will learn some things and you will deepen some friendships. That's what you started LIFESEARCH for anyway, isn't it?

STARTING A LIFESEARCH GROUP

The key ingredient to starting a LIFESEARCH group is *interest*. People are more likely to get excited about those things in which they are interested. People are more likely to join a group to study and to work on those areas of their lives in which they are interested.

Interest often comes when there is some itch to be scratched in a person's life, some anxiety to be soothed, or some pain to be healed.

Are persons interested in the topic of a LIFESEARCH book? Or, perhaps more important to ask, do they have needs in their lives that can be addressed using a LIFESEARCH book?

If you already have an existing group that finds interesting one of the topics covered by the LIFESEARCH books, go for it! Just keep in mind that LIFESEARCH is intended more as a small-group resource than as a class study textbook.

If you want to start a new group around LIFESEARCH, you can begin in one of two ways:

- You can begin with a group of interested people and let them choose from among the topics LIFESEARCH offers; or
- You can begin with one of the LIFESEARCH topics and locate people who are interested in forming a group around that topic.

What is the right size for a LIFESEARCH group? Well, how many persons do you have who are interested?

Actually, LIFESEARCH is intended as a *small-group* resource. The best size is between four and eight persons. Under four persons will make it difficult to carry out some of the group interactions. Over eight and not everyone will have a good opportunity to participate. The larger the group means the less time each person has to share.

If you have more than eight persons interested in your LIFESEARCH group, why not start two groups?

Or if you have a group larger than eight that just does not want to split up, then be sure to divide into smaller groups of no more than eight for discussion times. LIFESEARCH needs the kind of interaction and discussion that only happens in small groups.

How do you find out who is interested in LIFESEARCH? One good way is for you to sit down with a sheet of paper and to list the names of persons whom you think might be interested. Even better would be for you to get one or two other people to brainstorm names with you. Then start asking. Call people on the telephone. Or visit them in person. People respond more readily to personal invitations.

When you invite persons and they seem interested in LIFESEARCH, ask them if they will commit to attending all six sessions. Emergencies do arise, of course. However, the group's life is enhanced if all members participate in all sessions.

LIFESEARCH is as much a group experience as it is a time for personal learning.

As you plan to begin a LIFESEARCH group, you will need to answer these questions:

- **Who will lead the group?** Will you be the leader for all sessions? Do you plan to rotate leadership among the group members? Do you need to recruit an individual to serve as group leader?

- **Where will you meet?** You don't have to meet at a church. In fact, if you are wanting to involve a number of persons not related to your church, a neutral site might be more appropriate. Why not hold your meetings at a home? But if you do, make sure plans are made to hold distractions and interruptions to a minimum. Send the children elsewhere and put the answering machine on. Keep any refreshments simple.

- **How will you get the LIFESEARCH books to group members before the first session?** You will want to encourage members to read the first chapter in advance of the first session. Do you need to have an initial gathering some days before the first discussion session in order to hand out books and to take care of other housekeeping matters? Do you need to mail or otherwise transport the books to group members?

Most LIFESEARCH groups will last only long enough to work through the one LIFESEARCH book in which there is interest. Be open, however, to the possibility of either continuing your LIFESEARCH group as a support group around the life issue you studied or as a group to study another topic in the LIFESEARCH series.

TIPS FOR LIVELY DISCUSSIONS

TIP 1

Don't lecture. You are responsible for leading a discussion, not for conveying information.

TIP 2

Ask open-ended questions. Ask: How would you describe the color of the sky? Don't ask: Is the sky blue?

TIP 3

Allow silence. Sometimes, some people need to think about something before they say anything. The WRITTEN REFLECTIONS encourage this kind of thought.

TIP 4

Recognize when the silence has gone on long enough. Some questions do fall flat. Some questions exhaust themselves. Some silence means that people really have nothing more to say. You'll come to recognize different types of silences with experience.

TIP 5

If Plan A doesn't work to stimulate lively discussion, move on to Plan B. Each chapter in this LIFESEARCH book contains more discussion starters and group interaction ideas than you can use in an hour and a half. If something doesn't work, move on and try something else.

TIP 6

Let the group lead you in leading discussion. Let the group set the agenda. If you lead the group in the direction you want to go, you might discover that no one is following you. You are leading to serve the group, not to serve yourself.

Ask follow-up questions. If someone makes a statement or offers a response, ask: Why do you say that? Better yet, ask a different group member: What do you think of so-and-so's statement?

Do your own homework. Read the assigned chapter. Plan out possible directions for the group session to go based on the leader's helps in the text. Plan options in case your first plan doesn't work out. Know the chapter's material.

Know your group. Think about the peculiar interests and needs of the specific individuals within your group. Let your knowledge of the group shape the direction in which you lead the discussion.

Don't try to accomplish everything. Each chapter in this LIFESEARCH book offers more leader's helps in the form of DISCUSSION POINTS, GROUP INTERACTIONS, and other items than you can use in one session. So don't try to use them all! People become frustrated with group discussions that try to cover too much ground.

Don't let any one person dominate the discussion—including yourself. (See "Dealing With Group Problems," page 58.")

Encourage, but don't force, persons who hold back from participation. (See "Dealing With Group Problems," page 58.)

TAKING YOUR GROUP'S TEMPERATURE

How do you tell if your LIFESEARCH group is healthy? If it were one human being, you could take its temperature with a thermometer and discover whether body temperature seemed to be within a normal range. Taking the temperature of a group is more complex and less precise. But you can try some things to get a sense of how healthily your group is progressing.

✓ **Find out whether the group is measuring up to what the members expected of it.** During the CHECKING IN portion of the first session, you are asked to record what members say as they share why they came to this LIFESEARCH group. At a later time you can bring out that sheet and ask how well the LIFESEARCH experience measures up to satisfying why people came in the first place.

✓ **Ask how members perceive the group dynamics.** Say: On a scale from one as the lowest to ten as the highest, where would you rate the overall participation by members of this group? On the same scale where would you rate this LIFESEARCH group as meeting your needs? On the same scale where would you rate the "togetherness" of this LIFESEARCH group?

You can make up other appropriate questions to help you get a sense of the temperature of the group.

✓ **Ask group members to fill out an evaluation sheet on the LIFESEARCH experience.** Keep the evaluation form simple. One of the simplest forms leaves plenty of blank space for responding to three requests: (1) Name the three things you would want to do more of. (2) Name the three things you would want to do less of. (3) Name the three things you would keep about the same.

✓ **Debrief a LIFESEARCH session with one of the other participants.** Arrange ahead of time for a group member to stay a few minutes after a meeting or to meet with you the next day. Ask for direct feedback about what seemed to work or not work, who seems to be participating well, who seems to be dealing with something particularly troubling, and so forth.

✓ **Give group members permission to say when they sense something is not working.** As the group leader, you do not hold responsibility for the life of the group. The group's life belongs to *all* the members of the group. Encourage group members to take responsibility for what takes place within the group session.

✓ **Expect and accept that, at times, discussion starters will fall flat, group interaction will seem stilted, group members will be grumpy**. All groups have bad days. Moreover all groups go through their own life cycles. Although six sessions may not be enough time for your LIFESEARCH group to gel completely, you may find that after two or three sessions, one session will come when nothing seems to go right. That is normal. In fact, studies show that only those groups that first show a little conflict ever begin to move into deeper levels of relationship.

✔ **Sit back and observe.** In the middle of a DISCUSSION POINT or GROUP INTERACTION, sit back and try to look at the group as a whole. Does it look healthy to you? Is one person dominating? Does someone else seem to be withdrawn? How would you describe what you observe going on within the group at that time?

✔ **Take the temperature of the group—really!** No, not with a thermometer. But try asking the group to take its own temperature. Would it be normal? below normal? feverish? What adjective would you use to describe the group's temperature?

✔ **Keep a temperature record.** At least keep some notes from session to session on how you think the health of the group looks to you. Then after later sessions, you can look back on your notes from earlier sessions and see how your group has changed.

LifeSearch Group Temperature Record

Chapter 1
_____
_____
_____
_____

Chapter 2
_____
_____
_____
_____

Chapter 3
_____
_____
_____
_____

Chapter 4
_____
_____
_____
_____

Chapter 5
_____
_____
_____
_____

Chapter 6
_____
_____
_____
_____

DEALING WITH GROUP PROBLEMS

What do you do if your group just does not seem to be working out?

First, figure out what is going on. The ideas in "Taking Your Group's Temperature" (pages 56-57) will help you to do this. If you make the effort to observe and listen to your group, you should be able to anticipate and head off many potential problems.

Second, remember that the average LIFESEARCH group will only be together for six weeks—the average time needed to study one LIFESEARCH book. Most new groups will not have the chance to gel much in such a short period of time. Do not expect the kind of group development and nurture you might look for in a group that has lived and shared together for years.

Third, keep in mind that even though you are a leader, the main responsibility for how the group develops belongs to the group itself. You do the best you can to create a hospitable setting for your group's interactions. You do your homework to keep the discussion and interactions flowing. But ultimately, every member of the group individually and corporately bears responsibility for whatever happens within the life of the group.

However, if these specific problems do show up, try these suggestions:

✓ One Member Dominates the Group

• Help the group to identify this problem for itself by asking group members to state on a scale from one as the lowest to ten as the highest where they would rank overall participation within the group.

• Ask each member to respond briefly to a DISCUSSION POINT in a round robin fashion. It may be helpful to ask the member who dominates to respond toward the end of the round robin.

• Practice gate-keeping by saying, "We've heard from Joe; now what does someone else think?"

• If the problem becomes particularly troublesome, speak gently outside of a group session with the member who dominates.

✓ One Member Is Reluctant to Participate

• Ask each member to respond briefly to a DISCUSSION POINT in a round robin fashion.

• Practice gate-keeping for reluctant participants by saying, "Sam, what would you say about this?"

• Increase participation by dividing the larger group into smaller groups of two or three persons.

✓ The Group Chases Rabbits Instead of Staying With the Topic

• Judge whether the rabbit is really a legitimate or significant concern for the group to be discussing. By straying from your agenda, is the group setting an agenda more valid for their needs?

- Restate the original topic or question.

- Ask why the group seems to want to avoid a particular topic or question.

- If one individual keeps causing the group to stray inappropriately from the topic, speak with him or her outside of a session.

✓ Someone Drops Out of the Group

- A person might drop out of the group because his or her needs are not being met within the group. You will never know this unless you ask that person directly.

- Contact a person immediately following the first absence. Otherwise they are unlikely to return.

✓ The Group or Some of Its Members Remain on a Superficial Level of Discussion

- In a six-session study, you cannot necessarily expect enough trust to develop for a group to move deeper than a superficial level.

- Never press an individual member of a LIFESEARCH group to disclose anything more than he or she is comfortable doing in the group.

- Encourage an atmosphere of confidentiality within the group. Whatever is said within the group stays within the group.

✓ Someone Shares a Big, Dangerous, or Bizarre Problem

- LIFESEARCH groups are not therapy groups. You should not take on the responsibility of "fixing" someone else's problem.

- Encourage a member who shares a major problem to seek professional help.

- If necessary, remind the group about the need for confidentiality.

- If someone shares something that endangers either someone else or himself/herself, contact your pastor or a professional caregiver (psychologist, social worker, physician, attorney) for advice.

IF YOU'RE <u>NOT</u> LEADING THE GROUP

> Be sure to read this article if you are *not* the person with specific responsibility for leading your LIFESEARCH group.

If you want to get the most out of your LIFESEARCH group and this LIFESEARCH book, try the following suggestions.

✓ **Make a commitment to attend all the group sessions and participate fully.** An important part of the LIFESEARCH experience takes place within your group. If you miss a session, you miss out on the group life. Also, your group will miss what you would have added.

✓ **Read the assigned chapter in your LIFESEARCH book ahead of time.** If you are familiar with what the MAIN TEXT of the LIFESEARCH book says, you will be able to participate more fully in discussions and group interactions.

✓ **Try the activities suggested in BEFORE NEXT TIME.** Contributions you make to the group discussion based upon your experiences will enrich the whole group. Moreover, LIFESEARCH will only make a real difference in your life if you try out new skills and behaviors outside of the group sessions.

✓ **Keep confidences shared within the group.** Whatever anyone says within the group needs to stay within the group. Help make your group a safe place for persons to share their deeper thoughts, feelings, and needs.

✓ **Don't be a "problem" participant.** Certain behaviors will tend to cause difficulties within the life of any group. Read the article on "Dealing With Group Problems," on pages 58-59. Do any of these problem situations describe you? Take responsibility for your own group behavior, and change your behavior as necessary for the sake of the health of the whole group.

✓ **Take your turn as a group leader, if necessary.** Some LIFESEARCH groups will rotate group leadership among their members. If this is so for your LIFESEARCH group, accept your turn gladly. Read the other leadership articles in the back of this LIFESEARCH book. Relax, do your best, and have fun leading your group.

✓ **Realize that all group members exercise leadership within a group.** The health of your group's life belongs to all the group members, not just to the leader alone. What can you do to help your group become healthier and more helpful to its members? Be a "gatekeeper" for persons you notice are not talking much. Share a thought or a feeling if the discussion is slow to start. Back off from sharing your perspective if you sense you are dominating the discussion.

✓ **Take responsibility for yourself.** Share concerns, reflections, and opinions related to the topic at hand as appropriate. But keep in mind that the group does not exist to "fix" your problems. Neither can you "fix" anyone else's problems, though from time to time it may be appropriate to share insights on what someone else is facing based on your own experience and wisdom. Instead of saying, "What you need to do is . . ." try saying, "When I have faced a similar situation, I have found it helpful to . . ."

✓ **Own your own statements.** Instead of saying, "Everyone knows such and so is true," try saying "I believe such and so is true, because . . . ." Or instead of saying "That will never work," try saying, "I find it hard to see how that will work. Can anyone help me see how it might work?" Instead of saying, "That's dumb!" try saying, "I have a hard time accepting that statement because . . . ."

DOING LifeSearch IN ONE HOUR OR LESS

If you have already read "The LIFE-SEARCH Group Experience" on pages 49-51, you will have discovered that LIFESEARCH is designed for use in sessions of at least one and one-half hours in length. Or, if you have already tried to lead a LIFESEARCH session in a Sunday school class, you may have felt frustrated at so much material to cover in so little time. What do you do if you want to use LIFE-SEARCH in a Sunday school class or other setting that offers one hour or less?

You can choose from among three basic options:

—OPTION 1: Divide each session into two or more shorter sessions,

—OPTION 2: Abbreviate each session, or

—OPTION 3: Save LIFESEARCH for a longer time period than Sunday school allows.

✓ Dividing Sessions

If you want to cover all the material in the LIFESEARCH book but you do not have the luxury of one and one-half hour or longer sessions, you may want to divide each session as it appears in the book into shorter sessions. The downside is that your class or group will need more than six weeks to complete the study. Classes on a quarter structure might want to consider this option, however, and plan for twelve to thirteen weeks studying one LIFESEARCH book.

Once you choose to divide sessions, you will then have to decide at what point you are going to break off each session. Again, you have a couple of good possibilities:

—Break off wherever you happen to be at quitting time. Mark that place in your book, and resume there the following week.

—Assign approximate times to each learning option found in the marginal notes. If you have only forty-five minutes for your session, find and mark the point in your book where you will need to stop after roughly forty-five minutes of class time.

You will probably want to keep in some time at the beginning of each session for "checking in" as well as some time at the end for worship and prayer.

✓ Abbreviating Sessions

The option of abbreviating sessions will work best if you are limited to six sessions of one hour or less. Your dilemma will be to decide what material and learning options you will cover and what you will leave out.

Look at the learning options found in the marginal notes as items in a learning menu. Consider the goals of your group in choosing this LIFESEARCH book to study, the amount of time you have in your session, the interests of the individuals in your group, and the ways in which those individuals learn best. Not everyone learns best by means of reading and discussion! Some persons prefer to learn with more active and interactive learning methods. On the basis of these considerations, choose those learning options from the margin that will work best with your particular group within the time limitations you have.

The greatest danger leaders in this situation face is that they will be tempted to choose only those learning options they like or with which they feel comfortable. For the sake of the other members in your group, try stretching yourself and select learning options that will best fit *their* needs.

✓ Saving LIFESEARCH for Another Occasion

The curriculum planners who put together the LIFESEARCH approach believe that LIFESEARCH works best in time segments of at least one and one-half hours. This amount of time permits groups to develop *as groups*.

The content of your LIFESEARCH book is only part of what makes up your study experience. Yes, we hope that you will learn new knowledge and discover new skills to put into practice. But we also hope you will find nurture and support among the unique individuals who make up your group. The dynamics of your small community are important to your growth as a human being and as a Christian disciple.

Ideally, we would like to see your group continue meeting and helping one another beyond the time when you run out of materials from the six chapters of this book. You might want to try another LIFESEARCH study. Or, you might want simply to meet together weekly, biweekly, or monthly to talk about personal issues, struggles, and moments of growth concerning your LIFESEARCH topic.

Keep in mind that saving LIFESEARCH for a setting outside of Sunday morning and when you have more time than one hour may be what you and your group need to do. The choice of how you use LIFESEARCH belongs to you and your group.

OUR LifeSearch GROUP

Name Address Phone Number